SAN FRANCISCO
BAY AREA &
WINE COUNTRY

- - - - - - - - - - - - - - - - - -

ROAD
TRIPS

WITHDRAWN

This edition written and researched by

Sara Benson, Alison Bing, Beth Kohn, John A Vlahides

HOW TO USE THIS BOOK

Reviews

In the Destinations section:

All reviews are ordered in our authors' preference, starting with their most preferred option. Additionally:

Sights are arranged in the geographic order that we suggest you visit them and, within this order, by author preference.

Eating and Sleeping reviews are ordered by price range (budget, midrange, top end) and, within these ranges, by author preference.

Map Legend

Routes

- Trip Route
- Trip Detour
- Linked Trip
- Walk Route
- Tollway
- Freeway
- Primary
- Secondary
- Tertiary
- Lane
- Unsealed Road
- Plaza/Mall
- Steps
- Tunnel
- Pedestrian Overpass
- Walk Track/Path

Boundaries

- International
- State/Province
- Cliff

Population

- Capital (National)
- Capital (State/Province)
- City/Large Town
- Town/Village

Transport

- Airport
- Cable Car/ Funicular
- Parking
- Train/Railway
- Tram
- Underground Train Station

Trips

- Trip Numbers
- Trip Stop
- Walking Tour
- Trip Detour

Highway Route Markers

- US National Hwy
- US Interstate Hwy
- California State Hwy

Hydrography

- River/Creek
- Intermittent River
- Swamp/Mangrove
- Canal
- Water
- Dry/Salt/ Intermittent Lake
- Glacier

Areas

- Beach
- Cemetery (Christian)
- Cemetery (Other)
- Park
- Forest
- Reservation
- Urban Area
- Sportsground

Symbols In This Book

✔	Top Tips		Food & Drink
S	Link Your Trips		Outdoors
○	Tips from Locals		Essential Photo
↱	Trip Detour		Walking Tour
📖	History & Culture		Eating
👪	Family		Sleeping

◉	Sights	🛏	Sleeping
🏖	Beaches	✕	Eating
🏃	Activities	♟	Drinking
🎓	Courses	☆	Entertainment
☞	Tours	🛍	Shopping
🎉	Festivals & Events	ℹ	Information & Transport

These symbols and abbreviations give vital information for each listing:

☎	Telephone number	🐾	Pet-friendly
⊙	Opening hours	🚌	Bus
P	Parking	⛴	Ferry
⊝	Nonsmoking	🚊	Tram
✳	Air-conditioning	🚆	Train
@	Internet access	apt	apartments
🛜	Wi-fi access	d	double rooms
≋	Swimming pool	dm	dorm beds
🖊	Vegetarian selection	q	quad rooms
🍴	English-language menu	r	rooms
👪	Family-friendly	s	single rooms
		ste	suites
		tr	triple rooms
		tw	twin rooms

CONTENTS

PLAN YOUR TRIP

Welcome to San Francisco
Bay Area & Wine Country 5

San Francisco Bay Area &
Wine Country Map 6

San Francisco Bay Area &
Wine Country Highlights 8

San Francisco City Guide 10

Need to Know 12

ROAD TRIPS

1 San Francisco, Marin
& Napa Loop   4–5 Days 17

2 Napa
Valley   2–3 Days 25

3 Sonoma
Valley   2 Days   35

4 Russian River & the Bohemian
Highway   2 Days   43

DESTINATIONS

San Francisco 52

Marin County & the Bay Area 70

Marin Headlands 70

Sausalito 74

Sir Francis Drake Blvd & Around 78

Muir Woods National Monument 78

Bolinas 78

Point Reyes Station 79

Point Reyes National Seashore .. 80

Napa & Sonoma Wine Country 82

Napa Valley Wineries 82

Napa 83

Yountville 86

Oakville & Rutherford 88

St Helena 89

Calistoga & Around 91

Sonoma Valley Wineries 93

Sonoma & Around 94

Glen Ellen & Kenwood 97

Russian River Area Wineries 100

Sebastopol 102

Occidental & Around 105

Guerneville & Around 107

Healdsburg & Around 111

Bodega Bay 115

Sonoma Coast State Beach 117

Jenner 118

CALIFORNIA DRIVING GUIDE 120

Wine Country Vineyards stretch across rolling hills in Napa and Sonoma Valleys

WELCOME TO
SAN FRANCISCO BAY AREA & WINE COUNTRY

San Francisco is the anchor of California's most diverse region, even if earthquakes have shown it isn't rock solid. From exploring the rugged beaches of Marin County to floating down the isolated bends of the Russian River, from poking around (and through) the redwoods to picnicking beneath giant oaks, there's no shortage of natural places to explore and scenic roads to drive.

Then there is the wine and food... Many visitors seek out the iconic Napa Valley for cabernets and sparkling wines, but you can sip equally impressive vintages in Sonoma and Dry Creek. Then soak in some hot springs, where conversations start with, 'Hey, dude!' and end hours later.

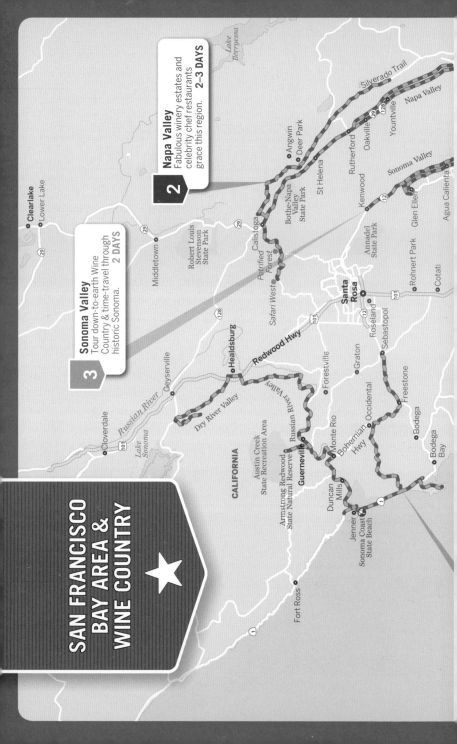

SAN FRANCISCO BAY AREA & WINE COUNTRY

★

2 Napa Valley
Fabulous winery estates and celebrity chef restaurants grace this region. **2–3 DAYS**

3 Sonoma Valley
Tour down-to-earth Wine Country & time-travel through historic Sonoma. **2 DAYS**

CALIFORNIA

Clearlake
Lower Lake
Lake Berryessa

Angwin
Deer Park

Silverado Trail
Napa Valley
Yountville
Oakville
Rutherford
St Helena
Bothe-Napa Valley State Park
Calistoga
Petrified Forest
Safari West
Robert Louis Stevenson State Park
Middletown

Kenwood
Sonoma Valley
Glen Ellen
Agua Caliente
Annadel State Park
Rohnert Park
Cotati

Santa Rosa
Roseland
Sebastopol
Graton
Forestville
Geyserville
Healdsburg
Redwood Hwy
Dry River Valley
Russian River Valley
Russian River
Lake Sonoma
Cloverdale

Occidental
Bohemian Hwy
Freestone
Bodega
Bodega Bay
Monte Rio
Guerneville
Duncan Mills
Austin Creek State Recreation Area
Armstrong Redwood State Natural Reserve
Jenner
Sonoma Coast State Beach
Fort Ross

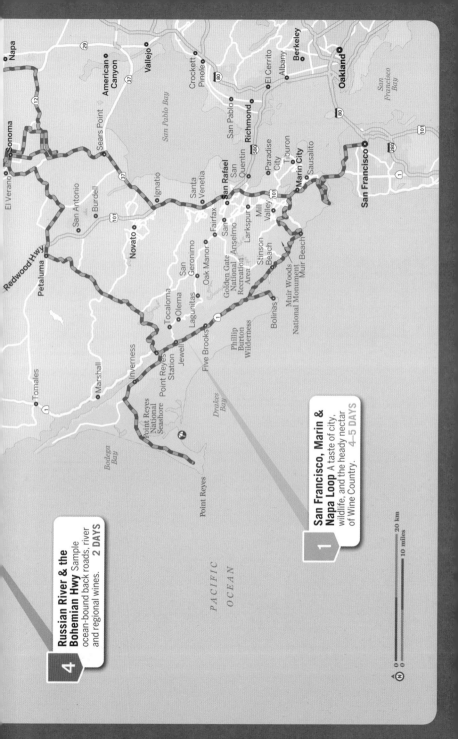

Napa (29)

Vallejo

American Canyon (37)

Crockett
Pinole (80)

El Cerrito

Berkeley

Oakland (80)

San Francisco Bay

(29) **Napa**

(12)

Sonoma
El Verano

Sears Point

San Pablo Bay

San Pablo
Richmond

San Quentin

Paradise City
Tiburon
Sausalito

(580)

(101)

(80)

(280)

(1)

San Francisco

Redwood Hwy

Petaluma

(37) Ignatio

Santa Venetia
San Rafael

Fairfax

San Anselmo

Larkspur

Mill Valley

Marin City

(101)

San Antonio
Burdell

(101)

Novato

Tocaloma
Olema
Lagunitas

San Geronimo
Oak Manor

Golden Gate National Recreation Area

Stinson Beach

Muir Woods National Monument
Muir Beach

Tomales

Marshall

Inverness

Point Reyes Station
Jewell
Five Brooks

(1)

Phillip Burton Wilderness

Bolinas

Point Reyes National Seashore

Drakes Bay

Bodega Bay

Point Reyes

PACIFIC OCEAN

4 Russian River & the Bohemian Hwy
Sample ocean-bound back roads, river and regional wines. **2 DAYS**

1 San Francisco, Marin & Napa Loop
A taste of city, wildlife, and the heady nectar of Wine Country. **4–5 DAYS**

N

0 ——— 20 km
0 ——— 10 miles

SAN FRANCISCO BAY AREA & WINE COUNTRY
HIGHLIGHTS
★

ABOVE: KANTOR/GETTY IMAGES ©

FEARGUS COONEY/GETTY IMAGES ©

Golden Gate Bridge (above)
Other suspension bridges
impress with engineering, but
none can touch the Golden
Gate Bridge for showmanship.
See it on Trip ①

Redwoods (left) California's
towering giants grow along
much of the coast, from
Big Sur north to the Oregon
border. See it on Trips ① ② ④

Wine Swaths of vineyards
carpet hillsides as far as
the eye can see, but it's
quality, not quantity, that
sets California's Wine
Country apart. See it on Trips
① ② ③ ④

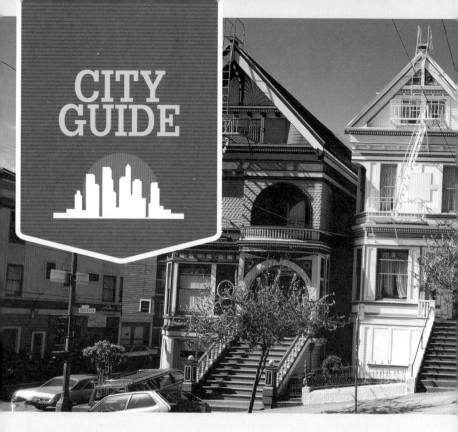

SAN FRANCISCO

Ride the clanging cable cars up unbelievably steep hills, snake down Lombard St's famous hairpin turns, cruise through Golden Gate Park and drive across the arching Golden Gate Bridge. Then go get lost in the creatively offbeat neighborhoods of California's capital of weird.

Getting Around

Avoid driving downtown. Cable cars are slow and scenic (single rides $6). MUNI streetcars and buses are faster but infrequent after 9pm (fares $2). BART (tickets from $1.75) run high-speed Bay Area trains. Taxis cost $2.75 per mile; meters start at $3.50.

Parking

Street parking is scarce and meter readers ruthless. Meters take coins, sometimes credit cards; central pay stations accept coins or cards. Overnight hotel parking averages $35 to $50; downtown parking garages start at $2.50 per hour or $25 per day.

THOMAS WINZ/GETTY IMAGES ©

San Francisco Victorian houses

Where to Eat

The Ferry Building, Mission District and
South of Market (SoMa) are foodie faves.
Don't miss the city's outdoor farmers
markets either. Head to North Beach
for Italian, Chinatown for dim sum, the
Mission District for Mexican, and the
Sunset or Richmond for pan-Asian.

Where to Stay

The Marina is near the family-friendly
waterfront and Fisherman's Wharf.
Downtown and Union Square are more
expensive, but conveniently located for
walking. Avoid the rough-edged Civic
Center and Tenderloin neighborhoods.

Useful Websites

San Francisco Travel (www.sanfrancisco.
travel) Destination info, events calendar and
accommodations bookings.

SF Station (www.sfstation.com) Nightlife,
restaurants, shopping and the arts.

Lonely Planet (www. lonelyplanet.com/usa/
san-francisco) Travel tips and travelers' forums.

Road Trip through San Francisco: 1
Destinations coverage: p52

For more, check out our
city and country guides.
www.lonelyplanet.com

NEED TO KNOW

CELL PHONES
The only foreign phones that will work in the USA are GSM multiband models. Network coverage is often spotty in remote areas (eg mountains, deserts).

INTERNET ACCESS
Wi-fi is available at most coffee shops and lodgings. Some accommodations have free guest computers. Cybercafes ($6 to $12 per hour) are common in cities.

FUEL
Gas stations are everywhere, except in national parks and remote areas. Expect to pay $4 to $5 per US gallon.

RENTAL CARS
Alamo (www.alamo.com)

Car Rental Express (www.carrentalexpress.com)

Simply Hybrid (www.simplyhybrid.com)

Zipcar (www.zipcar.com)

IMPORTANT NUMBERS
American Automobile Association (AAA; ☎877-428-2277)

Emergencies (☎911)

Highway conditions (☎800-427-7623)

Traffic updates (☎511)

Climate

- Desert, dry climate
- Dry climate
- Warm to hot summers, mild winters
- Warm to hot summers, cold winters

Arcata GO Apr–Oct

San Francisco GO Apr–Oct

Yosemite Village GO Apr–Oct

Los Angeles GO Apr–Oct

Palm Springs GO Dec–Apr

When to Go

High Season (Jun–Aug)
» Accommodations prices up 50% to 100%.

» Major holidays are even busier and more expensive.

» Summer is low season in the desert: temperatures exceed 100°F (38°C).

Shoulder Season (Apr–May & Sep–Oct)
» Crowds and prices drop, especially along the coast and in the mountains.

» Typically wetter in spring, drier in autumn.

» Milder temperatures and sunny, cloudless days.

Low Season (Nov–Mar)
» Accommodations rates drop in cities and by the coast.

» Many attractions open fewer days and shorter hours.

» Chilly temperatures and rainstorms; mudslides occasionally wash out coastal highways.

» In the mountains, carry tire chains; heavy snowfall closes higher-elevation roads.

» Winter is peak season in SoCal's desert regions.

Daily Costs

Budget: less than $75
» Camping: $20–40

» Meals in roadside diners and cafes: $10–20

» Graze farmers markets for cheaper eats

» Hit the beach and find 'free days' at museums

Midrange: $75–200
» Two-star motel or hotel double room: $75–150

» Meals in casual and midrange restaurants: $20–40

» Theme-park admission: $40–100

Top end: over $200
» Three-star lodging: from $150 per night in high season, more for ocean views

» Three-course meal in top restaurant: $75 plus wine

Eating

Roadside diners & cafes Cheap and simple; abundant only outside cities.

Beach shacks Casual burgers, shakes and seafood meals with ocean views.

National, state & theme parks Mostly so-so, overpriced cafeteria-style or deli picnic fare.

Vegetarians Food restrictions and allergies can usually be catered for at restaurants.

Eating price indicators represent the average cost of a main dish:

$	less than $10
$$	$10–$20
$$$	more than $20

Sleeping

Motels & hotels Ubiquitous along well-trafficked highways and in major tourist areas.

Camping & cabins Ranging from rustic campsites to luxury 'glamping' resorts.

B&Bs Quaint, romantic and pricey inns, found in most coastal and mountain towns.

Hostels Cheap and basic, but almost exclusively in cities.

Sleeping price indicators represent the average cost of a double room with private bathroom:

$	less than $100
$$	$100–$200
$$$	more than $200

Arriving in California

Los Angeles International Airport

Rental cars Major companies offer shuttles to off-airport lots.

Door-to-door shared-ride shuttles $16 to $25 one-way (reservations recommended).

Taxis $30 to $50 plus tip to Santa Monica, Hollywood or Downtown LA; 30mins to one hour.

Buses Take Shuttle C (free) to LAX City Bus Center or Metro FlyAway bus ($7) to Downtown LA.

San Francisco International Airport

Rental cars Take free AirTrain blue line to SFO Rental Car Center.

Door-to-door shared-ride shuttles $15 to $18 one-way (reservations recommended).

Taxis $35 to $50 plus tip to most San Francisco neighborhoods; 30 to 50 minutes.

Train BART ($8.10, 30 minutes to downtown SF) leaves every 20 minutes (take free AirTrain from any terminal to BART station).

Money

ATMs are widely available. Credit cards are accepted almost universally.

Tipping

Tipping is expected, not optional. Standard tips: 18% to 20% in restaurants; 15% for taxis; $1 per drink in bars; $2 per bag for porters.

Opening Hours

Banks 8:30am–4:30pm Mon–Fri, some to 5:30pm Fri, 9am–12:30pm Sat

Business hours (general) 9am–5pm Mon–Fri

Post offices 9am–5pm Mon–Fri, some 9am–noon Sat

Restaurants 7am–10:30am, 11:30am–2:30pm & 5–9:30pm daily, some later Fri & Sat

Shops 10am–6pm Mon-Sat, noon–5pm Sun (malls open later)

Useful Websites

Lonely Planet (www.lonelyplanet.com/usa/california) Destination info, hotel bookings, travelers' forums and more.

California Travel and Tourism Commission (www.visitcalifornia.com) Multilingual trip-planning guides and an events calendar.

For more, see Driving in California (p120)

Road Trips

1 **San Francisco, Marin & Napa Loop 4–5 Days**
A taste of city, an eyeful of wildlife, plus the heady nectar of Wine Country. (p17)

2 **Napa Valley 2–3 Days**
Fabulous winery estates and celebrity chef restaurants grace this grand wine-producing region. (p25)

3 **Sonoma Valley 2 Days**
Tour this down-to-earth part of Wine Country and time-travel through historic Sonoma. (p35)

4 **Russian River & the Bohemian Highway 2 Days**
Meander ocean-bound back roads, float in the river and sample regional wines. (p43)

Point Reyes National Seashore (p80)
GEORGE DIEBOLD/GETTY IMAGES ©

San Francisco, Marin & Napa Loop

1

Loop your way around the Bay Area, drinking in the sights of hilly San Francisco, the stunning wild vistas of Marin and the world-renowned wineries of Napa Valley and Sonoma County.

TRIP HIGHLIGHTS

65 miles
Point Reyes
Home to grazing deer, circling hawks and breaching whales

153 miles
Napa Valley
The premier wine-producing region in the country

Glen Ellen
Sonoma
9
Petaluma
Point Reyes Station
Olema
6

20 miles
Muir Woods
A canopy of massive ancient redwoods obscures the sun

4

2
START/ FINISH
San Francisco

Marin Headlands
Panoramic hilltop views from bay to breakers

8 miles

4–5 DAYS
253 MILES/407KM

GREAT FOR...

BEST TIME TO GO
April to October for dry and warmer days.

ESSENTIAL PHOTO
Views of Alcatraz, the Pacific Ocean, the Golden Gate Bridge and shimmering San Francisco unfold from Conzelman Rd.

BEST BIG TREES
Feel small under the rocketing redwoods of Muir Woods.

Lombard St, San Francisco Zigzag down 'the world's crookedest street'

1

San Francisco, Marin & Napa Loop

Begin by exploring the heady sights of cosmopolitan San Francisco before crossing north on the windswept passageway of the Golden Gate Bridge. From here, the scenery turns untamed, and Marin County's undulating hills, redwood forest and crashing coastline prove a welcome respite from urban living. Continue north to Napa and Sonoma Wine Country, basking in the warmer temperatures and tasting some of the best wines in the state.

① San Francisco (p52)

In two action-packed days, explore Golden Gate Park, spy on lolling sea lions at Fisherman's Wharf and saunter through the busy streets of Chinatown to the Italian sidewalk cafes in North Beach. Feast on an overstuffed burrito in the Mission District and then wander its mural-splashed alleys.

Queue up at Powell and Market Sts for a ride on a bell-clanging **cable car** (www.sfmta.com; ride $6), and then cruise to the infamous prison island of **Alcatraz** (☏415-981-7625;

LINK YOUR TRIP

 Napa Valley

From Napa, continue further north through Napa Valley along Hwy 29 for destination restaurants, a fabulous spa town and even more tempting wineries.

 Sonoma Valley

Venture north or south from Glen Ellen along Hwy 12 for low-key wine tasting and the historic sights clustered in downtown Sonoma.

www.alcatrazcruises.com; adult/child day $30/18, night $37/22; ⊘ferries depart Pier 33 every 30min 9am-3:55pm, plus 6:10pm & 6:45pm). In summer, book Alcatraz tickets online at least two weeks ahead.

At the foot of Market St, indulge your inner epicure at the food stalls in the **Ferry Building** (www.ferrybuildingmarketplace.com; Embarcadero; ⊘approximately 10am-6pm), and stop by its farmers market on Tuesday, Thursday and Saturday mornings year-round to wallow in the bounty of California-grown organic produce and gourmet prepared foods.

At the historic **Castro Theatre** (☏415-621-6120; www.castrotheatre.com; 429 Castro St; adult/child $11/8.50), the crowd goes wild when the giant organ rises from the floor and pumps out show tunes until the movie starts, and the sumptuous chandeliered decor complements a repertory of silver-screen classics.

The Drive » Aim north over the turret-topped Golden Gate Bridge, pausing to stroll around the Marin-side Vista Point area. Exit at Alexander Ave and bear left before swinging back under the highway to ascend the bayview ridgeline of Conzelman Rd. It's 2 miles to Hawk Hill, located just before the road becomes one-way.

TRIP HIGHLIGHT

② Marin Headlands (p70)

Near echoey WWII battery tunnels, bird-watchers should make a mandatory stop to hike up **Hawk Hill**. Thousands of migrating birds of prey soar here from late summer to early fall, straddling a windy ridge with views of Rodeo Lagoon all the way to Alcatraz.

Stay west on Conzelman Rd until it ends in about 2 miles and then bear left towards the bay. The third lighthouse built on the West Coast, the **Point Bonita Lighthouse** (www.nps.gov/goga/pobo.htm; off Field Rd; ⊘12:30-3:30pm Sat-Mon) FREE was completed in 1855, but after complaints about its performance in fog, it was scooted down to the promontory about 20 years later. Three afternoons a week you can cross through a dark rock tunnel – carved out with hand tools only – and traverse a steep half-mile trail to inspect the lighthouse beacon. A bouncy suspension bridge delivers you to the Fresnel lens tower, and harbor seals sun themselves on the rocks below.

The Drive » Continue north along the oceanview bluffs of Field Rd, joining westbound Bunker Rd (signed San Francisco) after passing the Marin Headlands Visitor Center. Pass through the timed one-way tunnel and turn left onto Alexander Ave towards Sausalito.

❸ Sausalito (p74)

Perfectly arranged on a secure little harbor on the bay, Sausalito's pretty houses tumble neatly down a green hillside into a well-heeled downtown, and much of the town affords uninterrupted views of San Francisco and Angel Island.

Just under the north tower of the Golden Gate Bridge, at East Fort Baker, families should stop by the **Bay Area Discovery Museum** (www. baykidsmuseum.org; 557 McReynolds Rd; admission $11; ⊙9am-5pm Tue-Sun;

🚼), an excellent hands-on activity museum specifically designed for children. Exhibits include a wave workshop, a small underwater tunnel and a large outdoor play area.

The Drive » Follow Hwy 101 north to Hwy 1, passing a stretch of Richardson Bay packed with funky houseboats. Ascend a mostly residential section of two-lane Hwy 1, and after 3 miles follow signs to Muir Woods via Panoramic Hwy.

TRIP HIGHLIGHT

❹ Muir Woods (p78)

Walking through an awesome stand of the world's tallest trees is an experience to be had only in Northern California and a small part of southern Oregon. The old-growth redwoods

➡ DETOUR:
CHEZ PANISSE

Start: ❶ **San Francisco**

The soul and anchor of Berkeley's 'Gourmet Ghetto,' Alice Waters' famed **Chez Panisse** (📞restaurant 510-548-5525, cafe 510-548-5049; www.chezpanisse.com; 1517 Shattuck Ave, Berkeley; restaurant prix-fixe dinner $65-100, cafe dinner $22-30; ⊙restaurant dinner Mon-Sat, cafe lunch & dinner Mon-Sat) gave birth to modern California cuisine and is a bucket-list destination for gourmands who prize fresh, local and organic ingredients. Upscale but unpretentious, its two dining rooms inhabit a welcoming Arts and Crafts house. The downstairs restaurant serves more formal prix-fixe meals, while the cafe upstairs is slightly less expensive. Reserve weeks ahead.

Cross the Bay Bridge to I-80, exiting at University Ave. At 2 miles, turn north onto Shattuck Ave.

at **Muir Woods** (www.nps. gov/muwo; adult/child $7/ free; ⊙8am-sunset) are the closest redwood stand to San Francisco. Logging plans were halted when congressman and naturalist William Kent bought a section of Redwood Creek, and in 1907 he donated 295 acres to the federal government. President Theodore Roosevelt made the site a national monument in 1908, the name honoring John Muir, naturalist and founder of environmental organization the Sierra Club.

Muir Woods can become quite crowded, especially on weekends. But even at busy times, a short hike will get you out of the densest crowds and onto trails with huge trees and stunning vistas. A lovely cafe serves local and organic goodies and hot drinks that hit the spot on foggy days.

The Drive » Head southwest on Muir Woods Dr (signed Muir Beach/Stinson Beach) and rejoin Hwy 1/Shoreline Hwy, winding north along this spectacularly scenic and curvy Pacific Ocean byway. Trace Bolinas Lagoon, where waterfowl prowl during low tide and harbor seals often frolic, and take the very first left after the lagoon. Go left onto Olema–Bolinas Rd into central Bolinas.

❺ Bolinas (p78)

Don't look for any signs directing you here. Residents from this

Sausalito

famously private town tore the road sign down so many times that state highway officials finally gave in and stopped replacing it years ago. Known as 'Jugville' during the Gold Rush days, the sleepy beachside community is home to writers, musicians and fisherfolk. Stroll along the sand from access points at Wharf Rd or Brighton Ave.

Hikers should veer off Olema–Bolinas Rd to Mesa Rd and follow it 5 miles to road's end at Palomarin Trailhead, the tromping-off point for coastal day hikes into the Point Reyes National Seashore. On a toasty day, pack some water and a towel and hightail it out from here

to **Bass Lake**, a popular freshwater swimming spot reached by way of a 3-mile hike skirting the coast. Another 1.5 miles of walking brings you to the fantastic flume of **Alamere Falls**, which tumbles 50ft off a cliff to the beach below.

The Drive » Return to Hwy 1 and continue 12 miles north through Olema Valley. Just past Olema, drive 23 miles west on Sir Francis Drake Blvd (towards Inverness), following the 'lighthouse' signs. Raptors perch on fence posts of historic cattle ranches, and the road bumps over rolling hills as it twists towards the sea.

- - - - - - - - - - -

TRIP HIGHLIGHT

6 Point Reyes (p79)

At the very end of Sir Francis Drake Blvd, and

jutting 10 miles out into the Pacific, this wild tip of land endures ferocious winds that can make it feel like the edge of the world. The **Point Reyes Lighthouse** (⊘ lighthouse 10am-4:30pm Fri-Mon, lens room 2:30-4pm Fri-Mon) **FREE** sits below the headlands at the base of over 300 stairs. Not merely a beautiful beacon site, it's also one of the best whale-watching spots along the coast, as gray whales pass the shore during their annual migration from Alaska to Baja. Gray-whale sightings tend to peak in mid-January and mid-March, with the season lasting from about January through to April. However, the occasional spout or spyhop of

21

humbacks and minkes can occur year-round.

Note that on weekends and holidays from late December through to mid-April, the road to the lighthouse is closed to private vehicles, and visitors must take a shuttle from Drakes Beach.

The Drive » Retrace Sir Francis Drake Blvd to Hwy 1 north and through the tiny village of Point Reyes Station. Soon after, go right onto Point Reyes–Petaluma Rd for 19 miles to Petaluma, stopping en route to sample brie at Marin French Cheese. At the railroad crossing, go right on Lakeville St, which becomes Hwy 116. Drive to Arnold Dr, turn right onto Petaluma Ave and pick up Hwy 12 north.

7 Glen Ellen (p97)

In Sonoma Valley, picnic like a rock star at the perpetually busy **BR Cohn** (www.brcohn. com; 15000 Sonoma Hwy; tasting $10, bottles $16-56; ⊙10am-5pm), whose founder managed '70s superband the Doobie Brothers before moving on to make outstanding organic olive oils and fine wines – including excellent cabernet sauvignon. In autumn, he throws benefit concerts, amid the olives, by the likes of Lynyrd Skynyrd and the Doobies.

The name **Little Vineyards** (www. littlevineyards.com; 15188 Sonoma Hwy; tastings $15, bottles $20-45; ⊙11am-4:30pm Thu-Mon; 🚻 🐕) fits at this family-owned small-scale winery. It's long on atmosphere, with a lazy dog to greet you and a weathered, cigarette-burned tasting bar, which Jack London drank at (before it was moved here). The tasting room is good for folks who dislike crowds, and there's good picnicking on the terrace with a vineyard view. The big reds include Syrah, Petite Sirah, Zinfandel, cab and several blends.

The Drive » Double back south on Hwy 12 and then east on Hwy 12/121. Make your way north on Hwy 29, exiting at Downtown Napa/First St. Follow the signs to the Oxbow Public Market.

8 Napa (p83)

Near the river in downtown Napa, the stands inside the **Oxbow Public Market** (www. oxbowpublicmarket.com; 644 1st St; ⊙9am-7pm Mon & Wed-Sat, to 8pm Tue, 10am-5pm Sun; 🚻 🛒) offer everything from fresh-roasted organic coffee to cranberry baguette sandwiches with pea shoots and fontina. Sample a beef frank at the counter of **Five Dot Ranch** (www.fivedotranch. com), an all-natural beef purveyor with a holistic, sustainable, open-pasture program combined with low-stress handling. The family has been raising California livestock for seven generations. Top it off a couple of stands over with the funky, creative and organic flavors of **Three Twins Ice Cream** (www. threetwinsicecream.com) – try the Strawberry Je Ne Sais Quoi, where the creaminess is cut with an unexpected dash of balsamic vinegar.

The Drive » Leaving Napa, take picturesque Hwy 29 (St Helena Hwy) 12 miles north to Oakville, driving past the Napa Valley foodie destination of Yountville.

WILDLIFE WATCHING

Want to see marine wildlife in Marin? Here are a few choice spots suggested by Anne Bauer, Director of Education at the **Marine Mammal Center** (p72).

» Point Reyes National Seashore (Chimney Rock & Point Reyes Lighthouse) for gray whales

» Bolinas (Duxbury Reef, Bolinas Lagoon), Marin Headlands (around Point Bonita) and Point Reyes National Seashore (Limantour Estero) for harbor seals

» Point Reyes National Seashore (Sea Lion Overlook) for sea lions

9 Napa Valley (p82)

The huge, corporate-owned winery of **Robert Mondavi** (www.robertmondaviwinery.com; 7801 Hwy 29, Oakville; tasting & tour $20-55, bottles $25-150; ⊙10am-5pm) draws oppressive crowds, but if you know nothing about wine, the worthwhile tours provide excellent insight into wine making. Otherwise, skip it – unless you're here for one of the wonderful summer concerts, ranging from classical and jazz to R&B and Latin.

A half-mile south, just after the Oakville Grocery, take a left onto Oakville Cross Rd and drive 2.5 miles, passing through vineyards

WINE TASTING 101

Even if you know nothing about wine, you can enjoy it with gusto. Inhale the wine's aroma by burying your nose deep in the glass. Swirl it and look at its color before letting it hit every part of your tongue. It's OK not to drain every glass (in fact, it'll dull your taste buds if you do). Use the containers on the counter to empty your glass and prepare for your next taste. You won't be offending anyone!

to Silverado Trail. For hilltop views and food-friendly wines, head south another 2.5 miles to visit chef-owned **Robert Sinskey** (☎707-944-9090; www.robertsinskey.com; 6320 Silverado Trail, Napa; tastings $25, incl tour $50-75, bottles $28-95; ⊙10am-4:30pm), whose discreetly dramatic tasting room of stone, redwood and teak resembles a small cathedral. The winery

specializes in organically grown Pinot, Merlot and Cabernet, great Alsatian varietals, Vin Gris, Cabernet Franc and dry Rosé, and small bites accompany the *vino*.

The Drive » Continue south on Silverado Trail to Napa, picking up southbound Hwy 121 (Sonoma)/Hwy 29 (Vallejo) and turning right as it merges into westbound Hwy 12 (Sonoma). Stay on Hwy 121 until Hwy 37, and take it west. From Hwy 101, it's 20 miles back to San Francisco via the Golden Gate Bridge.

Napa Valley

2

The birthplace of modern-day Wine Country is famous for regal cabernet sauvignons, château-like wineries and fabulous food. Expect to be wined, dined and tucked between crisp linens.

TRIP HIGHLIGHTS

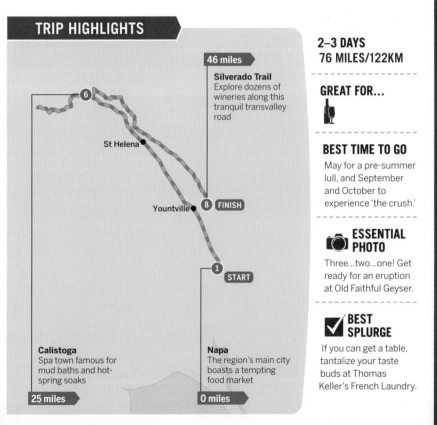

46 miles

Silverado Trail
Explore dozens of wineries along this tranquil transvalley road

St Helena

6

Yountville **8** FINISH

1 START

Calistoga
Spa town famous for mud baths and hot-spring soaks

25 miles

Napa
The region's main city boasts a tempting food market

0 miles

2–3 DAYS
76 MILES/122KM

GREAT FOR...

BEST TIME TO GO
May for a pre-summer lull, and September and October to experience 'the crush.'

ESSENTIAL PHOTO
Three...two...one! Get ready for an eruption at Old Faithful Geyser.

BEST SPLURGE
If you can get a table, tantalize your taste buds at Thomas Keller's French Laundry.

Napa Valley Swaths of vineyards carpet hillsides

2 Napa Valley

America's premier viticulture region has earned its reputation among the world's best. Rolling hills, dotted with century-old oaks, turn the color of lion's fur under the summer sun and swaths of vineyards carpet hillsides as far as the eye can see. Hundreds of wineries inhabit Napa Valley, but it's quality, not quantity, that sets the region apart — it competes with France and doubles as an outpost of San Francisco's top-end culinary scene.

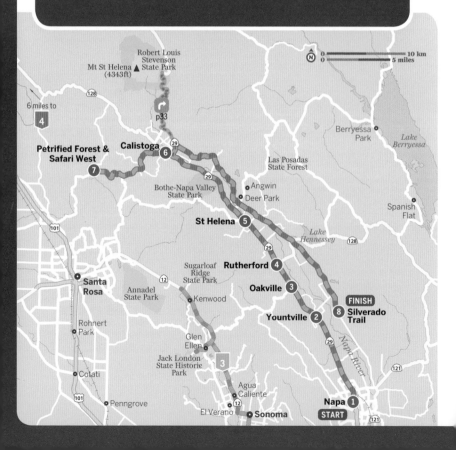

TRIP HIGHLIGHT

❶ Napa (p83)

The valley's workaday hub was once a nothing-special city of storefronts, Victorian cottages and riverfront warehouses, but booming real-estate values caused an influx of new money that has transformed Napa into a growing city of arts and food. Its number-one attraction, the **Oxbow Public Market** (www.oxbowpublicmarket.com; 644 1st St; ◷9am-7pm Mon & Wed-Sat, to 8pm Tue, 10am-5pm Sun; 🚼🚲) showcases all things culinary – from produce stalls to kitchen stores to fantastic edibles. It's foodie central, with

LINK YOUR TRIP

3 **Sonoma Valley**

For lower-key wineries and Sonoma's early California historical sites, Hwy 12/121 is the main connector between the Napa and Sonoma Valleys.

4 **Russian River & the Bohemian Highway**

From Calistoga, continue west on Hwy 128 for river dips, rural wineries and wildlife watching along rugged undeveloped coastline.

an emphasis on seasonal and regional ingredients, grown sustainably. Graze your way through this gourmet market and plug into the Northern California food scene. Standouts include fresh oysters, Venezuelan cornbread sandwiches, excellent Cal-Mexican and certified-organic ice cream. Tuesday is locals night, with many discounts. On Tuesday and Saturday mornings, there's a farmers market. Friday nights bring live music.

West of downtown, scrap-metal sheep graze Carneros vineyards at 217-acre **Di Rosa Art + Nature Preserve** (☎707-226-5991; www.dirosaart.org; 5200 Hwy 121; admission $5, tours $12-15; ◷10am-4pm Wed-Sun), a stunning collection of Northern California art displayed indoors in galleries and outdoors in sculpture gardens. Reservations are recommended for tours.

The Drive » From Napa, Yountville is 9 miles north on Hwy 29, a divided four-lane road surrounded by vineyards and framed by low hills.

❷ Yountville (p87)

This one-time stagecoach stop is now a major foodie destination, with more Michelin stars per capita than any other American town. There are some good inns here,

but it's deathly boring at night. You stay in Yountville to drink with dinner without having to drive afterward – but make reservations or you might not eat!

Ma(i)sonry (☎707-944-0889; www.maisonry.com; 6711 Washington St; ◷10am-6pm Sun-Thu, to 7pm Fri & Sat) occupies a 1904 stone house, now transformed into a rustic-modern showplace for furniture, art and wine. The garden is a swank postdinner fireside gathering spot for *vino*.

Yountville's modernist 40,000-sq-ft **Napa Valley Museum** (☎707-944-0500; www.napavalleymuseum.org; 55 Presidents Circle; adult/child $5/2.50; ◷10am-5pm Wed-Mon), off California Dr, chronicles cultural history and showcases local paintings, and has good picnicking outside.

The Drive » Go north to Oakville via another 4 miles of vineyard vistas on Hwy 29, which slims to two lanes just outside of Yountville. Tracks for the Napa Valley Wine Train line the west side of the road.

❸ Oakville (p88)

But for its famous grocery, you'd drive through the tiny settlement of Oakville (population 71) and never know you'd missed it. This is the middle of the grapes – vineyards sprawl in every direction.

The behemoth **Robert Mondavi Winery** ([J]888-766-6328; www. robertmondaviwinery.com; 7801 Hwy 29; tours $15-25, bottles $19-150; ⊙10am-5pm) is somewhat of a corporate-winery experience and you can expect a lot of company. That said, the grounds are gorgeous and it offers a good menu of tours and tastings for those who are new to wine. The winery also uses careful environmental practices in its farming, managing 1000 acres of naturally farmed vineyards.

The Drive » Rows of grapevines recede into the distance as you continue 2 miles north on Hwy 29.

- - - - - - - - - - - -

❹ Rutherford (p88)

Another blip of a town, Rutherford (population 164) is more conspicuous, with its wineries putting it on the map. The valley views are spectacular at **Mumm Napa** ([J]800-686-6272; www.mummnapa.com;

8445 Silverado Trail; tasting $18-40; ⊙10am-4:45pm), which makes respectable sparkling wines that you can sample while seated on a vineyard-view terrace. No appointment necessary, and you can dodge crowds by paying $40 extra for the reserve-tasting terrace. Check the website for discount tasting coupons.

Meandering paths wind through the magical gardens and fruit-bearing orchards of **Frog's Leap** ([J]707-963-4704; www.frogsleap.com; 8815 Conn Creek Rd; tastings $15, incl tour $20, bottles $22-42, ⊙by appointment; [icons]) – pick peaches in July – surrounding an 1884 barn and farmstead with cats and chickens. But more than anything, it's the vibe that's wonderful: casual and down-to-earth, with a major emphasis on *fun*. Sauvignon Blanc is its best-known wine, but the Merlot merits attention, and all are

organic. There's also a dry, restrained Cabernet, atypical in Napa.

Round Pond ([J]888-302-2575; www.roundpond. com; 875 Rutherford Rd; tastings $25, bottles $30-1680; ⊙by appointment) tantalizes with fantastic food pairings on a vineyard-view stone patio. We especially love the olive-oil and wine-vinegar tastings, which are included with guided tours of the olive mill ($45).

The Drive » St Helena is another 4 miles north on Hwy 29, though you may be slowing to a crawl before hitting the first stoplight in the center of town.

- - - - - - - - - - - -

❺ St Helena (p89)

You'll know you're arriving here when traffic halts. St Helena (ha-*lee*-na) is the Rodeo Dr of Napa, with fancy boutiques lining Main St (Hwy 29). The historic downtown is good for a stroll, with great window-shopping, but parking is next to impossible on summer weekends.

Owned by Bill Clinton's former ambassador to Austria, **Hall** ([J]707-967-2626; www.hallwines.com; 401 St Helena Hwy; tastings $30, bottles $22-80; ⊙10am-5:30pm; [icon]) specializes in Cabernet Franc, Sauvignon Blanc, Merlot and Cabernet Sauvignon. There's a cool abstract-sculpture garden and a lovely picnic area shaded by mulberry trees (with

NAPA VALLEY WINERIES

Cab is king in Napa. No varietal captures imaginations like the fruit of the Cabernet Sauvignon vine – Bordeaux is the French equivalent – and no wine fetches a higher price. Napa farmers can't afford *not* to grow Cabernet. Other heat-loving varietals, such as Sangiovese and Merlot, also thrive here.

Napa's wines merit their reputation among the world's finest – complex, with luxurious finishes. Napa wineries sell many 'buy-and-hold' wines, versus Sonoma's 'drink-now' wines.

DRIVING IN NAPA VALLEY

» Napa Valley is 30 miles long and 5 miles wide at its widest point (the city of Napa), 1 mile at its narrowest (Calistoga). Two roads run north–south: Hwy 29 (St Helena Hwy) and the more scenic Silverado Trail, a mile east. Drive up one, and down the other.

» The American Automobile Association determined Napa Valley to be America's eighth-most congested rural vacation destination. Summer and fall weekend traffic is unbearable, especially on Hwy 29 between Napa and St Helena. Plan accordingly.

» Cross-valley roads that link Silverado Trail with Hwy 29 – including Yountville, Oakville and Rutherford crossroads – are bucolic and get less traffic. For scenery, the Oakville Grade and rural Trinity Rd (which leads southwest to Hwy 12 in Sonoma Valley) are narrow, curvy and beautiful – but treacherous in rainstorms. Mt Veeder Rd leads through pristine countryside west of Yountville.

» Police watch like hawks for traffic violators. Don't drink and drive.

wines by the glass) at this Leadership in Energy & Environmental Design–gold-certified winery – California's first (tours $50, including barrel tastings).

The **Silverado Museum** (📞707-963-3757; www.silveradomuseum.org; 1490 Library Lane; ⏱noon-4pm Tue-Sat) FREE contains a fascinating collection of Robert Louis Stevenson memorabilia. In 1880, the author – then sick, penniless and unknown – stayed in an abandoned bunkhouse at the old Silverado Mine on Mt St Helena with his wife, Fanny Osbourne; his novel *The Silverado Squatters* is based on his time there. To reach Library Lane, turn east off Hwy 29 at the Adams St traffic light and cross the railroad tracks.

Hushed and regal, the 1889 stone château of the **Culinary Institute of**

America at Greystone (📞707-967-2320; www.ciachef.edu/california; 2555 Main St; mains $25-29, cooking demonstration $20; ⏱restaurant 11:30am-9pm, cooking demonstrations 1:30pm Sat & Sun) houses a gadget- and cookbook-filled culinary shop; an upscale restaurant and a new cafe; weekend cooking demonstrations; and wine-tasting classes by luminaries in the field, including Karen MacNeil, author of *The Wine Bible*.

The Drive » Trees begin to reappear on the landscape,

breaking up the vineyard views as you head 8 miles north on Hwy 29.

TRIP HIGHLIGHT

❻ Calistoga (p91)

The least gentrified town in Napa Valley feels refreshingly simple, with an old-fashioned main street lined with shops, not boutiques, and diverse characters wandering the sidewalks. Calistoga is synonymous with the mineral water bearing its name, bottled here since 1924, and its springs and geysers have

BOOKING WINERY APPOINTMENTS

Because of strict county zoning laws, many Napa wineries cannot legally receive drop-in visitors; unless you've come strictly to buy, you'll have to call ahead. This is *not* the case with all wineries. We recommend booking one appointment and planning your day around it.

LOCAL KNOWLEDGE
DALIA CEJA,
CEJA VINEYARDS

Indian Springs Spa
(📞707-942-4913; www.
indianspringscalistoga.com; 1712 Lincoln Ave,
Calistoga; ⊘ by appointment 9am-8pm) **is
the perfect place to relax either as a
couple or with a group of friends. You
can take a bath with mud infused
with lavender and chamomile, and
afterwards take a dip in the Olympic-
size natural mineral pool. On a chilly
fall day, swimming in the pool – the
temperature reaches about 100°F at
one end – is my number-one favorite
thing to do.**

Top: Castello di Amorosa
Left: Mud therapy
Right: Old Faithful Geyser

earned it the nickname the 'hot springs of the West.' Plan to visit one of the town's spas, where you can indulge in the local specialty: a hot-mud bath, made of the volcanic ash from nearby Mt St Helena.

It took 14 years to build the perfectly replicated 12th-century Italian castle **Castello di Amorosa** (☎707-967-6272; www.castellodiamorosa.com; 4045 Hwy 29; tasting $19-29, incl guided tour $34-75, bottles $20-125; ⏰9.30am-6pm, to 5pm Nov-Feb), complete with moat, hand-cut stone walls, ceiling frescoes by Italian artisans, Roman-style cross-vault brick catacombs, and a torture chamber with period equipment. You can taste without an appointment, but this is one tour worth taking. Wines include some respectable Italian varietals, including a velvety Tuscan blend.

Calistoga's mini-version of Yellowstone, the **Old Faithful Geyser** (☎707-942-6463; www.oldfaithfulgeyser.com; 1299 Tubbs Lane; adult/child $14/8; ⏰9am-6pm, to 5pm Nov-Mar; 👶) shoots boiling water 60ft to 100ft into the air, every 30 minutes. The vibe is pure roadside Americana, with folksy hand-painted interpretive exhibits, picnicking and a little petting zoo, where you can come nose-to-nose with llamas. It's north of

Calistoga, via Hwy 128 west to Tubbs Lane, and discount coupons are available online.

The Drive » Backtrack east on Hwy 128 and go 4 miles west on forested and curvy Petrified Forest Rd.

- - - - - - - - - -

❼ Petrified Forest & Safari West

Three million years ago, a volcanic eruption at nearby Mt St Helena blew down a stand of redwoods between Calistoga and Santa Rosa. The trees fell in the same direction, away from the blast, and were covered in ash and mud. Over the millennia, the mighty giants' trunks turned to stone. Gradually the overlay eroded, exposing them, and the first stumps of **Petrified Forest** (📞707-942-6667; www.petrifiedforest.org; 4100 Petrified Forest Rd; adult/child $10/5; ⏱9am-7pm summer, to 5pm winter) were discovered in 1870. A monument marks Robert Louis Stevenson's 1880 visit. He describes it in *The Silverado Squatters*. Check online for 10%-off coupons.

Giraffes in Wine Country? Whadya know! Just 4 miles west (Petrified Forest Rd becomes Porter Creek Rd), **Safari West** (📞707-579-2551; www.safariwest.com; 3115 Porter Creek Rd; adult $72-98, child 3-12 $32; 👪) covers 400 acres and protects zebras, cheetahs and other exotic animals, which mostly

CALISTOGA SPAS

Calistoga is famous for hot-spring spas and mud-bath emporiums, where you're buried in hot mud and emerge feeling supple, detoxified and enlivened. (The mud is made with volcanic ash and peat; the higher the ash content, the better the bath.)

Packages take 60 to 90 minutes and cost $70 to $90. You start semisubmerged in hot mud, then soak in hot mineral water. A steam bath and blanket-wrap follow. The treatment can be extended with a massage, increasing the cost to $130 and up.

Baths can be taken solo or, at some spas, as couples. Variations include thin, painted-on clay-mud wraps (called 'fango' baths, good for those uncomfortable sitting in mud), herbal wraps, seaweed baths and various massage treatments. Discount coupons are sometimes available from the visitors center. Reservations essential at all spas, especially on summer weekends.

Indian Springs Spa (p30) The longest continually operating spa and original Calistoga resort has concrete mud tubs and mines its own ash. Treatments include use of the huge, hot-spring-fed pool.

Spa Solage (📞707-226-0825; www.solagecalistoga.com; 755 Silverado Trail; ⏱by appointment 8am-8pm) Chichi, austere, top-end spa, with couples' rooms and a fango-mud bar for DIY paint-on treatments. Also has zero-gravity chairs for blanket wraps, and a clothing-optional pool.

Dr Wilkinson's Hot Springs Resort (📞707-942-4102; www.drwilkinson.com; 1507 Lincoln Ave; ⏱by appointment 10am-3.30pm) Operational for 50 years, 'the doc' uses more peat in its mud.

Mount View Spa (📞707-942-5789; www.mountviewhotel.com; 1457 Lincoln Ave; ⏱by appointment 9am-9pm) Traditional full-service, 12-room spa, good for clean-hands gals who prefer painted-on mud to submersion.

Calistoga Spa Hot Springs (📞707-942-6269; www.calistogaspa.com; 1006 Washington St; ⏱by appointment 8:30am-4:30pm Tue-Thu, to 9pm Fri-Mon; 👪) Traditional mud baths and massage at a motel complex with two huge **swimming pools** (⏱10am-9pm) where kids can play while you soak (pool passes $25).

DETOUR:
ROBERT LOUIS STEVENSON STATE PARK

Start: 6 Calistoga

Eight miles north of Calistoga via curvaceous Hwy 29, the long-extinct volcanic cone of Mt St Helena marks the Napa Valley's end. Encircled within undeveloped **Robert Louis Stevenson State Park** (☎707-942-4575; www.parks.ca.gov), the crest often gets snow in winter. It's a strenuous 5-mile climb to the peak's 4343ft summit, but what a view – 200 miles on a clear winter's day. Check conditions before setting out. Also consider 2.2-mile one-way Table Rock Trail (go south from the summit parking area) for drop-dead valley views. Temperatures are best in wildflower season, February to May; fall is prettiest, when the vineyards change colors.

The park includes the site of the Silverado Mine where Stevenson and his wife honeymooned in 1880.

roam free. See them on a guided three-hour safari in open-sided jeeps; reservations required. You'll also walk through an aviary and lemur condo. The reservations-only cafe serves lunch and dinner. If you're feeling adventurous, stay overnight in nifty canvas-sided **tent cabins** (cabins incl breakfast $225-325), right in the preserve.

The Drive » Return east back to Calistoga and drive 1 mile south on Hwy 29/128 and 1 mile north on Lincoln Ave to the Silverado Trail. Journey 21 miles southeast along lovely Silverado Trail, lined with row after row of grapevines.

- - - - - - - - - -

TRIP HIGHLIGHT

8 Silverado Trail

The Napa Valley winery jackpot, Silverado Trail runs from Calistoga to Napa and counts

approximately three-dozen wineries along its bucolic path. At the northernmost reaches of the Silverado Trail, and breaking ranks with Napa snobbery, the party kids at **Lava Vine** (☎707-942-9500; www.lavavine. com; 965 Silverado Trail; tasting $10; ⏰10am-5pm, appointment suggested; 🚹🐾) take a lighthearted approach to their seriously good wines, all paired with small bites, including some hot off the barbecue. Children and dogs play outside, while you let your guard down in the tiny tasting room. Bring a picnic.

One of Napa's oldest wineries, unfussy **Regusci** (☎707-254-0403; www.regusciwinery.com; 5584 Silverado Trail; tasting $25-30, incl tour $30-60, bottles $36-140; ⏰10am-5pm) dates to the late 1800s, with 173 acres of vineyards unfurling around a

century-old stone winery that makes Bordeaux-style blends. Located along the valley's quieter eastern side, it's a good bet when traffic up-valley is bad. No appointments are necessary, and the oak-shaded picnic area is lovely.

Like a modern-day Persian palace, **Darioush** (☎707-257-2345; www. darioush.com; 4240 Silverado Trail; tastings $18-40, bottles $40-95; ⏰10:30am-5pm) ranks high on the fabulosity scale, with towering columns, Le Corbusier furniture, Persian rugs and travertine walls. Though known for Cabernet, Darioush also bottles Chardonnay, Merlot and Shiraz, all made with 100% of their respective varietals. Reserve in advance for its wine-and-cheese pairings.

Sonoma Valley

3

Flanked by sun-drenched hills and vast vineyard landscapes, the bountiful roadside farms and unassuming top-notch wineries along this trip make for a relaxing excursion.

TRIP HIGHLIGHTS

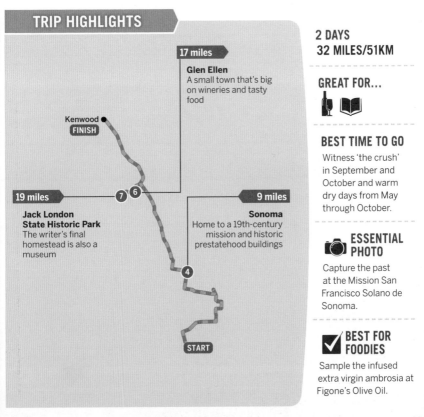

17 miles

Glen Ellen
A small town that's big on wineries and tasty food

Kenwood
FINISH

19 miles

Jack London State Historic Park
The writer's final homestead is also a museum

7 6

9 miles

Sonoma
Home to a 19th-century mission and historic prestatehood buildings

4

START

2 DAYS
32 MILES/51KM

GREAT FOR...

BEST TIME TO GO
Witness 'the crush' in September and October and warm dry days from May through October.

ESSENTIAL PHOTO
Capture the past at the Mission San Francisco Solano de Sonoma.

BEST FOR FOODIES
Sample the infused extra virgin ambrosia at Figone's Olive Oil.

Sonoma Valley Explore vineyards and farms in this folksy, bucolic region

3 Sonoma Valley

Locals call it 'Slow-noma.' Unlike fancy Napa, nobody in folksy Sonoma cares if you drive a clunker and vote Green. Anchoring the bucolic, 17-mile-long Sonoma Valley, the town of Sonoma makes a great jumping-off point for exploring Wine Country – it's only an hour from San Francisco – and has a marvelous sense of place, with storied 19th-century historical sights surrounding the state's largest town square.

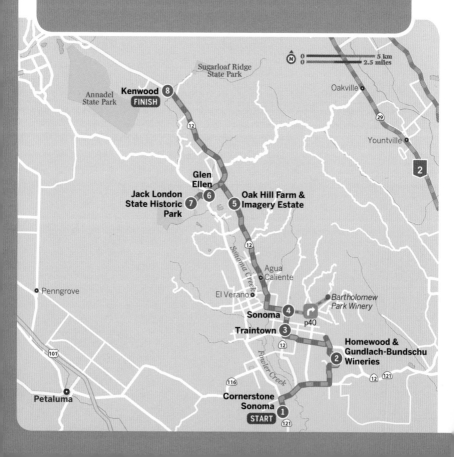

➊ Cornerstone Sonoma

There's nothing traditional about **Cornerstone Sonoma** (☎707-933-3010; www.cornerstonegardens.com; 23570 Arnold Dr, Hwy 121; ⏰10am-4pm; 🚻) FREE, which showcases the work of renowned avant-garde landscape designers. Set aside an hour to stroll through the thought-provoking and conceptual gardens. Look for the enormous blue chair at road's edge.

The Drive ≫ Go north on Hwy 121 and follow it for 3 miles as it bears east. Turn south on Burndale Rd. Homewood winery is on your left, at the flagpole.

LINK YOUR TRIP

2 **Napa Valley**
For upscale wineries, spa resorts and top notch restaurants, Hwy 12/121 is the main connector between the Napa and Sonoma Valleys.

4 **Russian River & the Bohemian Highway**

From Kenwood, go west on Hwy 12 for summertime river dips, delightful wineries and rambles in redwood forest or pristine Pacific beach.

➋ Homewood & Gundlach-Bundschu Wineries

A stripy rooster named Steve chases dogs in the parking lot of **Homewood** (☎707-996-6353; www.homewoodwinery.com; 23120 Burndale Rd, at Hwy 121/12; tastings $5, bottles $22-42; ⏰10am-4pm; 🐾), a down-home winery whose motto sums it up: 'Da redder, da better.' The tasting room is a garage, and the winemaker crafts standout ports and Rhône-style Grenache, Mourvèdre and Syrah. Ask about 'vertical tastings,' and sample wines from the same vineyards but different years. From Homewood, go north on Burndale Rd, jog left briefly onto Napa Rd and then right onto Denmark St.

One of Sonoma Valley's oldest and prettiest wineries, **Gundlach-Bundschu** (☎707-939-3015; www.gunbun.com; 2000 Denmark St; tastings $10-15, bottles $22-45; ⏰11am-4:30pm) looks like a storybook castle. Founded in 1858 by Bavarian immigrant Jacob Gundlach, it's now at the cutting edge of sustainability. Signature wines are Rieslings and Gewürztraminers, but 'Gun-Bun' was the first American winery to produce 100% Merlot. Tours of the 2000-barrel cave ($20) are available

by reservation. Down a winding lane and with a small lake, it's also pleasant for picnicking and hiking.

The Drive ≫ Follow Denmark St back to Napa Rd, and go west to Hwy 12. Drive Hwy 12/Broadway north a quarter mile to Traintown.

➌ Traintown

If you're traveling with young children, make a beeline to **Traintown** (☎707-938-3912; www.traintown.com; 20264 Broadway; ⏰10am-5pm daily summer, Fri-Sun only mid-Sep–late May; 🚻). A miniature steam engine makes 20-minute loops ($5.75), and there are vintage amusement-park rides ($2.75 per ride), including a carousel and a Ferris wheel.

The Drive ≫ Drive north on Hwy 12/Broadway about one mile.

TRIP HIGHLIGHT

➍ Sonoma (p94)

Kick back for a few hours in Sonoma's town square, with tree-lined paths and a playground, surrounded by shops, restaurants and tasting rooms. Comprising multiple sites, the **Sonoma State Historic Park** (☎707-938-9560; www.parks.ca.gov; adult/child $3/2; ⏰10am-5pm) is a must-see for California history buffs. The **Mission San Francisco Solano de Sonoma** (E Spain St), at the

SAN FRANCISCO BAY AREA & WINE COUNTRY **3** SONOMA VALLEY

plaza's northeast corner, was built in 1823, in part to forestall the Russian coastal colony at Fort Ross from moving inland. The mission was the 21st and final California mission, and the only one built during the Mexican period (the rest were founded by the Spanish). The not-to-be-missed chapel dates from 1841.

The adobe **Sonoma Barracks** (E Spain St) was built by Vallejo between 1836 and 1840 to house Mexican troops, but it became the capital of a rogue nation on June 14, 1846, when American settlers, of varying sobriety, surprised the guards and declared an independent 'California Republc' [sic] with a homemade flag featuring a blotchy bear. The US took over the republic a month later, but abandoned the barracks during the Gold Rush, leaving Vallejo to turn them into (what else?) a winery in 1860.

Walk just round the corner to stock up for an afternoon picnic. Known for its dry-jack cheeses (made here since the 1930s), **Vella Cheese Co** (☎707-928-3232; www. vellacheese.com; 315 2nd St E; ◷9:30am-6pm Mon-Sat) also makes delectable Mezzo Secco with cocoa powder–dusted rind.

The Drive » Head north on Hwy 12 for about five miles to Oak Hill Farm along tree-lined vineyards.

- - - - - - - - - - - - -

❺ Oak Hill Farm & Imagery Estate

At the southern end of Glen Ellen, **Oak Hill Farm** (☎707-996-6643; www. oakhillfarm.net; 15101 Sonoma Hwy; ◷11am-6pm Wed-Sun Apr-Dec; 🚻) contains acres upon acres of organic flowers and produce, hemmed in by lovely steep oak and manzanita woodland. The farm's Red Barn Store is a historic dairy barn filled with handmade wreaths, herbs and organic

goods reaped from the surrounding fields. Try the heirloom tomatoes, pumpkins and blue plums.

Just farther north on Sonoma Hwy, **Imagery Estate** (☎707-935-4515; www.imagerywinery.com; 14335 Sonoma Hwy; tastings $10-20; ◷10am-4:30pm; 🚻🍷) boasts bottle labels designed by local artists; the art changes with each vintage and varietal. A gallery houses the entire collection of artwork – over 200 pieces with interpretations of the winery's signature Parthenon symbol. The heavy-sweet Viognier and Moscato are popular, and all wines are certified biodynamic.

The Drive » Continue half a mile north before dipping 1.5 miles west and then south on Arnold Dr to the Jack London Village complex.

- - - - - - - - - - - - -

TRIP HIGHLIGHT

❻ Glen Ellen (p97)

Try not to drool as you compare chocolates with

THE BEAR FLAG REPUBLIC

Sonoma has a rich history. In 1846 it was the site of a second American revolution, this time against Mexico, when General Mariano Guadalupe Vallejo deported all foreigners from California, prompting outraged American frontiersmen to occupy the Sonoma Presidio and declare independence. They dubbed California the Bear Flag Republic after the battle flag they'd fashioned.

The republic was short-lived. The Mexican–American War broke out a month later, and California was annexed by the US. The revolt gave California its flag, which remains emblazoned with the words 'California Republic' beneath a muscular brown bear. Vallejo was initially imprisoned, but ultimately returned to Sonoma and played a major role in the region's development.

varying percentages of cacao at **Wine Country Chocolates Tasting Bar** (☏707-996-1010; www.winecountrychocolates.com; 14301 Arnold Dr; ◷10am-5pm). Pick up some champagne- or Cabernet-infused truffles for the drive, or do your best to save them for gifts.

If you're new to wine, take a crash course in winemaking and biodynamic vineyard practices at **Benziger** (☏888-490-2739; www.benziger.com; 1883 London Ranch Rd; tasting $15-20, tram tour adult/under 21yr $25/10, bottles $15-80; ◷10am-5pm, tram tours 11:30am-3:30pm;

🚹🐾). The worthwhile, nonreservable tour includes an open-air tram ride through biodynamic vineyards, and a four-wine tasting. Afterward, you can check out the caves – and the Cabernets. You'll also learn about the difference between organic and biodynamic farming – biodynamic systems work to achieve a balance with the entire ecosystem, going beyond organic practices. Kids love the peacocks. The large-production wine's OK (head for the reserves), but the tour's the draw.

The Drive » From Benziger, go half a mile farther west on London Ranch Rd to reach Jack London State Historic Park.

TRIP HIGHLIGHT

7 Jack London State Historic Park

Napa has Robert Louis Stevenson, but Sonoma's got Jack London. This 1400-acre **park** (☏707-938-5216; www.jacklondonpark.com; 2400 London Ranch Rd, Glen Ellen; per car $10, tour adult/child $4/2; ◷9:30am-5pm; 🚹) traces the last years of the author's life.

Changing occupations from Oakland fisherman

DETOUR: BARTHOLOMEW PARK

Start: 4 Sonoma

The top close-to-town outdoors destination is 375-acre **Bartholomew Park Winery** (☎707-939-3026; www.bartpark.com; 1000 Vineyard Lane, Sonoma), off Castle Rd to the east of town, where you can picnic beneath giant oaks and hike 3 miles of trails, with hilltop vistas to San Francisco. There's also a good winery and small museum. The Palladian Villa, at the park's entrance, is a turn-of-the-20th-century replica of the original residence of Count Haraszthy, a pioneering Sonoma vintner. It's open noon to 3pm, Saturdays and Sundays, and operated by the **Bartholomew Foundation** (☎707-938-2244).

to Alaska gold prospector to Pacific yachtsman – and novelist on the side – London (1876–1916) ultimately took up farming. He bought Beauty Ranch in 1905 and moved there in 1910. With his second wife, Charmian, he lived and wrote in a small cottage while his mansion, Wolf House, was under construction. On the eve of its completion in 1913, it burned down. The disaster devastated London, and although he toyed with rebuilding, he died before construction got underway. His widow built the House of Happy Walls, which has been preserved as a museum. It's a half-mile walk from

there to the remains of Wolf House, passing London's grave along the way. Other paths wind around the farm to the cottage where he lived and worked. Miles of hiking trails (some open to mountain bikes) weave through oak-dotted woodlands, between 600ft and 2300ft elevation.

The Drive » Drive east back to Hwy 12, and 3 miles north for the Wildwood Farm and Sculpture Garden.

- - - - - - - - - - -

8 Kenwood (p97)

Gardeners shouldn't miss **Wildwood Farm and Sculpture Garden** (☎707-833-1161, 888-833-4181; www.

wildwoodmaples.com; 10300 Sonoma Hwy; ⊙10am-4pm Wed-Sun, 10am-3pm Tue), where abstract outdoor art sits between exotic plants and Japanese maples.

Family-run **Figone's Olive Oil** (☎707-282-9092; www.figoneoliveoil.com; 9580 Sonoma Hwy; ⊙11am-5pm) grows its own olives and presses extra-virgin olive oil. Take a break from wine tasting and sample the infused citrus oils (think Meyer lemons or blood oranges) and exquisite balsamics.

A cult favorite, supercool winery **Kaz** (☎707-833-2536; www.kazwinery.com; 233 Adobe Canyon Rd; tastings $5, bottles $20-48; ⊙11am-5pm Fri-Mon; ⊕🎨) is about blends – whatever's in the organic vineyards goes into the wine – and they're blended at crush, not during fermentation. Expect lesser-known varietals like Alicante Bouchet and Lenoir, and a worthwhile Cabernet-Merlot blend. Kids can sample grape juice, then run around the playground out back, while you sift through LPs and pop your favorites onto the turntable. Crazy fun.

Russian River & the Bohemian Highway

4

In western Sonoma County, tour organic wineries, stately redwood forests, ribbons of undulating road and the serene Russian River, then ogle seals and whales along the coast.

TRIP HIGHLIGHTS

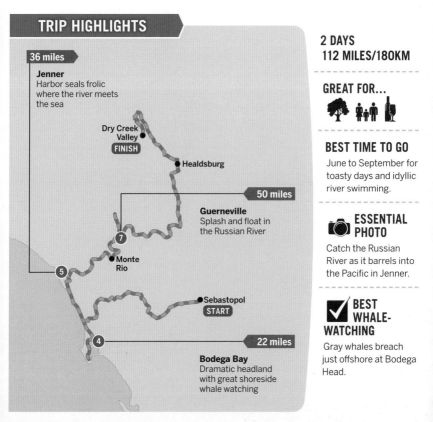

36 miles

Jenner
Harbor seals frolic where the river meets the sea

Dry Creek Valley
FINISH

Healdsburg

50 miles

Guerneville
Splash and float in the Russian River

7

Monte Rio

5

Sebastopol
START

4

22 miles

Bodega Bay
Dramatic headland with great shoreside whale watching

**2 DAYS
112 MILES/180KM**

GREAT FOR...

BEST TIME TO GO
June to September for toasty days and idyllic river swimming.

ESSENTIAL PHOTO
Catch the Russian River as it barrels into the Pacific in Jenner.

BEST WHALE-WATCHING
Gray whales breach just offshore at Bodega Head.

Goat Rock Beach Rent kayaks for seal spotting

4 Russian River & the Bohemian Highway

Lesser-known West Sonoma County was formerly famous for its apple farms and vacation cottages. Lately vineyards are replacing the orchards, and the Russian River has now taken its place among California's important wine appellations for superb pinot noir. 'The River,' as locals call it, has long been a summertime weekend destination for Northern Californians, who come to canoe, wander country lanes, taste wine, hike redwood forests and live at a lazy pace.

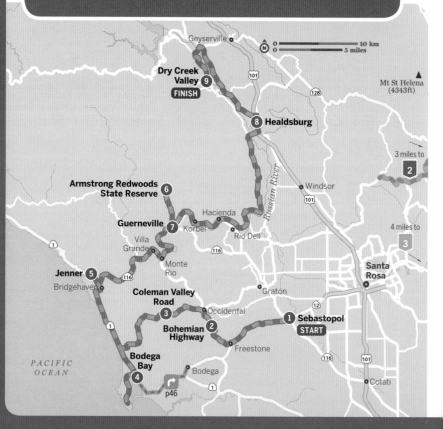

① Sebastopol (p102)

Grapes have replaced apples as the new cash crop, but Sebastopol's farm-town identity remains rooted in the apple – evidence: the much-heralded summertime Gravenstein Apple Fair. The town center feels suburban because of traffic, but a hippie tinge and quirky shops such as a beekeeping store give it color.

Just north off Bodega Ave, prepare to giggle at the wacky **Patrick Amiot sculptures** (www.patrickamiot.com;) gracing front yards along Florence Ave. Fashioned from recycled materials, a hot-rodding rat, hectic waitress and a witch in midflight are a few of the oversized and demented lawn ornaments parading along the street.

The Drive » From the central intersection of Hwys 116 and 12, head west on Bodega Ave (signed Bodega Bay) for 6 miles, passing apple orchards en route to tiny Freestone.

② Bohemian Highway

Running north from the town of **Freestone**, the pastoral 10-mile Bohemian Hwy tours past farmland and then constricts through stands of redwoods, ending at the Russian River in tiny Monte Rio. At the southern end, the crossroads of Freestone isn't much more than just that, though the former railway stop boasts a crazy-popular bakery, a cute country store and a Japanese-inspired spa specializing in unique cedar treatments. Stop by for a tasting at Joseph Phelps, **Freestone Vineyards Guest Center** (☎707-874-1010; www.josephphelps.com; cnr Bodega & Bohemian Hwys; tastings $20-35; ⏱11am-5pm), one of the rare spots in the area that produces excellent Pinot Noir, and with biodynamic farming methods to boot.

Just over 3 miles north, **Occidental** (p106) is a haven of artists, back-to-the-landers and counterculturalists. Historic 19th-century buildings line a single main street, easy to explore in an hour. On Fridays, meet the whole community at the detour-worthy **farmers market** (www.occidentalfarmersmarket.com; ⏱4pm-dusk Fri Jun-Oct), with musicians, craftspeople and – the star attraction – **Gerard's Paella** (www.gerardspaella.com) of TV-cooking-show fame.

The Drive » In the center of Occidental, turn west onto well-signed Coleman Valley Rd.

③ Coleman Valley Road

Sonoma County's most scenic drive isn't through the grapes, but along 10 miles of winding West County byway, from Occidental to the sea. It's best in the late morning, after the fog has cleared and the sun's behind you. First you'll pass through redwood forests and lush valleys where Douglas firs stand draped in sphagnum moss – an eerie sight in the fog. The real beauty shots lie further ahead, when the road ascends 1000ft hills, dotted with gnarled oaks and craggy rock formations, with the Pacific unfurling below.

The Drive » The road ends at coastal Hwy 1 in the midst of Sonoma Coast State Beach, which stretches 17 miles from Bodega Head to just north of Jenner. From Hwy 1, head 2.5 miles south, then west onto Eastshore Rd. Go right at the stop sign onto Bay Flat Rd and along the harbor until road's end.

---

⑤ LINK YOUR TRIP

2 Napa Valley

In Dry Creek Valley, take Canyon Rd and then head east on Hwy 128 to visit the showcase wineries and destination restaurants of Napa Valley.

3 Sonoma Valley

From Sebastopol, head east on Hwy 12 for Sonoma Valley wine tasting and the historical sights around Sonoma Plaza.

④ Bodega Bay (p115)

The town of Bodega Bay sits at the southernmost section of the glorious **Sonoma Coast State Beach** (p117; ☎707-875-3483; www.parks.ca.gov), a series of beaches separated by several beautiful rocky headlands. Some beaches are tiny, hidden in little coves, while others stretch far and wide or are connected by vista-studded coastal hiking trails that wind along the bluffs. At the tip of a peninsula, the windy crown jewel of **Bodega Head** rises 265ft above sea level, with dreamy views out onto the open ocean and excellent whale watching and kite flying.

The Drive » Return to Hwy 1 and trace the coastline 12 miles north to Goat Rock Rd in Jenner.

⑤ Jenner (p118)

In the small village of Jenner, the Russian River merges with the ocean. At the end of Goat Rock Rd, bear left for **Blind Beach**, where the mass of Goat Rock looms above and splendid Arched Rock seems to hover offshore. Then double back to **Goat Rock Beach**, where a harbor seal colony sits at the river's mouth and pups are born from March to August. The best way to see the seals is by kayak, and most of the year you can rent them at the river's edge.

The Drive » After crossing the last bridge over the Russian River before it joins the sea, go east on Hwy 116/River Rd, a well-paved country road sandwiched between the river and abrupt hills speckled with weather-beaten wooden barns. In Guerneville, turn left at the sign for Armstrong Woods.

⑥ Armstrong Redwoods State Reserve

Soaring redwood trees and leaf-carpeted forest floor create a profound silence that spreads for 805 acres at **Armstrong Redwoods State Reserve** (☎707-869-2015; www.parks.ca.gov; 17000 Armstrong Woods Rd; per vehicle $8; ⊙8am-sunset;). The *Return of the Jedi* Ewok-village chase scene was filmed here; speed-pods zoomed between the columnar trunks of these 265ft giants. The tranquil, disabled-accessible Discovery Trail passes Armstrong Tree, a 1400-year-old behemoth.

The Drive » Return 3 miles south to River Rd. Jog west one block to Church St and follow it one block south to the beach.

⮕ DETOUR: BLOODTHIRSTY BIRDS OF BODEGA

Start: ④ Bodega Bay

Bodega Bay has the enduring claim to fame as the setting for Alfred Hitchcock's *The Birds.* Although special effects radically altered the actual layout of the town, you still get a good feel for the supposed site of the farm owned by Mitch Brenner (played by Rod Taylor). The once-cozy Tides Restaurant, where much avian-caused havoc occurs in the movie, is still there, but since 1962 it has been transformed into a vast restaurant complex. Venture 5 miles inland (south on Hwy 1) to the tiny town of **Bodega** and you'll find two icons from the film: the schoolhouse and the church. Both stand just as they did in the movie – a crow overhead may make the hairs rise on your neck.

Russian River

TRIP HIGHLIGHT

7 Guerneville (p107)

The colorful, oddball main street of Guerneville bustles with life, as tourists and locals alike cruise the storefronts and galleries and dip in to the cafes, restaurants and bars.

There's nothing quite like floating in the cool river here on a scorching summer day. Head to **Johnson's Beach** (☏707-869-2022; www. johnsonsbeach.com; 16241 First St; admission free, kayak & canoe per hr/day $10/30; ⊙10am-6pm May-Sep; ⋒) to rent kayaks and canoes that you launch from and return to the beach.

About 2.5 miles east of central Guerneville, the ivy-draped brick winery at **Korbel** (☏707-824-7000; www.korbel.com; 13250 River Rd; ⊙10am-5pm; ⏮) gets jammed on weekends as folks come from all around to sip the champagnes it's been making since 1882.

The Drive ››› Continue east on River Rd, forking left onto Westside Dr about 2.5 miles after Korbel. The two-lane road passes numerous wineries, and opens up to views of 4343ft-tall Mt St Helena to the northeast.

Cross Dry Creek and Hwy 101 to reach Healdsburg in 12 miles.

8 Healdsburg (p111)

Once a sleepy agricultural town best known for its Future Farmers of America parade, Healdsburg has emerged as northern Sonoma County's culinary capital. Foodie-scenester restaurants and cafes, wine-tasting rooms and fancy boutiques line **Healdsburg Plaza**, the town's sun-dappled central square (bordered by Healdsburg Ave and Center, Matheson and

Plaza Sts). Traffic grinds to a halt on summer weekends, when second-home-owners and tourists jam downtown. Old-timers aren't happy with the Napa-style gentrification, but at least Healdsburg retains its historic look, if not its once-quiet summers. It's best visited weekdays – stroll tree-lined streets, sample locavore cooking and soak up the NorCal flavor.

Tasting rooms surround the plaza and free summer concerts are held on Tuesday afternoons. And on a hot day, take a dip in the Russian River at **Healdsburg Veterans Memorial Beach** (☎707-433-1625; www.sonoma-countyparks.org; 13839 Healdsburg Ave; parking $7; ⊙7am-sunset; 🐾), where lifeguards are on duty on weekends in summer.

The Drive » From Healdsburg Plaza, drive 1 mile north on Healdsburg Ave and then west onto Dry Creek Rd, a fast-moving main thoroughfare; it's about 10 miles on to Truett-Hurst. To reach the wineries on West Dry Creek Rd, a parallel and undulating country lane, take Yoakim Bridge Rd.

- - - - - - - - - -

❾ Dry Creek Valley (p101)

A wine-growing region hemmed in by 2000ft-high mountains, Dry Creek Valley is relatively warm, ideal for Sauvignon Blanc, Zinfandel and, in some places, Cabernet Sauvignon.

Dry Creek's newest biodynamic winery, **Truett-Hurst Vineyards** (☎707-433-9545; www.truetthurst.com; 5610 Dry Creek Rd; tastings $5-10; ⊙10am-5pm; 🐾) has terrific old-vine zins, standout Petite Sirah and Russian River Pinots at the handsome, contemporary tasting room, and you can meander to the creek where salmon spawn in autumn.

An early leader in organics, the 19th-century farm of **Preston Vineyards** (☎707-433-3372; www.prestonvineyards.com; 9282 W Dry Creek Rd; tasting $5, refundable with purchase, bottles $24-38; ⊙11am-4:30pm; 🐾) feels like old Sonoma County. Weathered picket fencing frames the 19th-century farmhouse-turned-tasting room with candy-colored walls. The signature is citrusy Sauvignon Blanc, but try the Rhône varietals and small-lot wines.

Atop the valley's north end, caves are built into the hillside at always-fun **Bella Vineyards** (☎707-473-9171; www.bellawinery.com; 9711 W Dry Creek Rd; tasting $10, bottles $25-42; ⊙11am-4:30pm; 🐾). The focus is on Zin and Syrah, but there's terrific Rosé.

Destinations

San Francisco (p52)
Get to know the world capital of weird from the inside out, from mural-lined alleyways named after poets to clothing-optional beaches on a former military base.

Marin County & the Bay Area (p70)
The region surrounding San Francisco encompasses a bonanza of natural vistas and wildlife.

Napa & Sonoma Wine Country (p82)
Rolling hills, dotted with century-old oaks, turn the color of lion's fur under the summer sun and swaths of vineyards carpet hillsides as far as the eye can see in Wine Country.

Russian River (Trip 4)
ROBERT HOLMES/GETTY IMAGES ©

San Francisco

*Get to know the world
capital of weird from the
inside out, from mural-lined
alleyways named after poets
to clothing-optional beaches
on a former military base.*

But don't be too quick to dismiss San Francisco's wild ideas. Biotech, gay rights, personal computers, cable cars and organic fine dining were once considered outlandish too, before San Francisco introduced these underground ideas into the mainstream decades ago. San Francisco's morning fog erases the boundaries between land and ocean, reality and infinite possibility.

Rules are never strictly followed here. Golden Gate Bridge and Alcatraz are entirely optional – San Franciscans mostly admire them from afar – leaving you free to pursue inspiration through Golden Gate Park, past flamboyantly painted Victorian homes and through Mission galleries. Just don't be late for your sensational, sustainable dinner: in San Francisco, you can find happiness and eat it too.

History

Oysters and acorn bread were prime dinner options in the Mexico-run Ohlone settlement of San Francisco circa 1848 – but a year and some gold nuggets later, Champagne and chow mein were served by the bucket. Gold found in nearby Sierra Nevada foothills turned a sleepy 800-person village into a port city of 100,000 prospectors, con artists, prostitutes and honest folk – good luck telling them apart in the city's 200 saloons.

Panic struck when Australia glutted the market with gold in 1854. Rioters burned waterfront 'Sydney-Town' before turning on SF's Chinese community, who from 1877 to 1945 were restricted to living and working in Chinatown by anti-Chinese exclusion laws. Chinese laborers were left with few employment options besides dangerous work building railroads for San Francisco's robber barons, who dynamited, mined and clear-cut their way across the Golden West, and built Nob Hill mansions above Chinatown.

But the city's grand ambitions came crashing down in 1906, when earthquake and fire reduced the city to rubble. Theater troupes and opera divas performed for free amid smoldering ruins, and reconstruction hummed along at an astounding rate of 15 buildings per day.

During WWII, soldiers accused of insubordination and homosexuality were dismissed in San Francisco, as though that would teach them a lesson. Instead San Francisco's counterculture thrived, with North Beach jazz and Beat poetry. When the Central Intelligence Agency (CIA) tested LSD on the willing volunteer and *One Flew Over the Cuckoo's Nest* author Ken Kesey, he slipped some into Kool-Aid and kicked off the psychedelic '60s.

The Summer of Love brought free food, love and music to the Haight, and pioneering gay activists in the Castro helped elect Harvey Milk as San Francisco supervisor –

San Francisco's hilly streets

America's first out gay official. When San Francisco witnessed devastating losses from HIV/AIDS in the 1980s, the city rallied to become a global model for epidemic treatment and prevention.

San Francisco's unconventional thinking spawned the web in the 1990s, until the dot-com bubble burst in 2000. But risk-taking SF continues to float outlandish new ideas – social media, mobile apps, biotech. Congratulations: you're just in time for San Francisco's next wild ride.

- -

◉ Top Sights

Alcatraz   Historic Site

See pages 19, 58

Golden Gate Bridge   Landmark

(www.goldengatebridge.org/visitors; off Lincoln Blvd; northbound free, southbound toll $6, billed electronically to vehicle's license plate; 🚌28, all Golden Gate Transit buses) Hard to believe the Navy almost nixed SF's signature art-deco landmark by architects Gertrude and Irving Murrow and engineer Joseph B Strauss. Photographers, take your cue from Hitchcock: seen from **Fort Point** (☏415-556-1693; www.nps.gov/fopo; Marine Dr; ◷10am-5pm Fri-Sun; 🅿; 🚌28) **FREE**, the 1937 bridge induces a thrilling case of vertigo. Fog aficionados prefer Marin's Vista Point, watching gusts billow through bridge cables like dry ice at a Kiss concert. For the full effect, hike or bike the 2-mile span.

★ DON'T MISS: GOLDEN GATE PARK

When San Franciscans refer to 'the park,' there's only one that gets the definite article. Everything they hold dear is in Golden Gate Park (http://sfrecpark.org; 👶👹; 🚌5, 18, 21, 28, 29, 33, 44, 71, Ⓜ N) 🐾, including free spirits, free music, Frisbee and bison.

The park offers 7.5 miles of bicycle trails, 12 miles of equestrian trails, an archery range, fly-casting pools, four soccer fields and 21 tennis courts. Sundays, when JFK Dr closes to traffic around 9th Ave, don't miss roller disco and lindy-hopping in the park. Other times, catch these park highlights:

MH de Young Museum (☏415-750-3600; http://deyoung.famsf.org/; 50 Hagiwara Tea Garden Dr; adult/child $10/6, discount with MUNI ticket $2, 1st Tue of month free, online booking fee $1 per ticket; ◷9:30am-5:15pm Tue-Sun, to 8:45pm Fri Apr-Nov; 🚌5, 44, 71, Ⓜ N) Follow sculptor Andy Goldsworthy's artificial earthquake fault in the sidewalk into Herzog + de Meuron's faultlessly sleek, copper-clad building that's oxidizing green to blend into the park. Don't be fooled by the de Young's camouflaged exterior: shows here boldly broaden artistic horizons, from Oceanic ceremonial masks and Bulgari jewels to California photographer Anthony Friedkin's 1970s portraits of gay liberation.

California Academy of Sciences (☏415-379-8000; www.calacademy.org; 55 Music Concourse Dr; adult/child $34.95/24.95, discount with MUNI ticket $3; ◷9:30am-5pm Mon-Sat, 11am-5pm Sun; 🅿👶; 🚌5, 6, 31, 33, 44, 71, Ⓜ N) Architect Renzo Piano's landmark, LEED-certified green building houses 38,000 weird and wonderful animals, with a four-story rainforest and split-level aquarium under a 'living roof' of California wildflowers. After the penguins nod off to sleep, the wild rumpus starts at kids'-only Academy Sleepovers and over-21 NightLife Thursdays, when rainforest-themed cocktails encourage strange mating rituals among shy first dates.

Japanese Tea Garden (☏tea ceremony reservations 415-752-1171; www.japaneseteagardensf. com; 75 Hagiwara Tea Garden Dr; adult/child $7/2, before 10am Mon, Wed & Fri free; ◷9am-6pm Mar-Oct, to 4:45pm Nov-Feb; 🅿👶; 🚌5, 44, 71, Ⓜ N) Since 1894, this 5-acre garden has blushed with cherry blossoms in spring, turned flaming red with maple leaves in fall, and lost all track of time in the meditative Zen Garden. The 100-year-old bonsai grove is the legacy of founder Makoto Hagiwara, who tended them until his family's forced deportation to WWII Japanese American internment camps, and spent decades afterwards restoring these priceless miniature evergreens. Don't miss green tea and fortune cookies (invented for the garden's opening) at the tea pavilion.

THREE CHINATOWN ALLEYS THAT MADE HISTORY

» **Waverly Place** (🚌30, 🚋California St, Powell-Mason) After the 1906 earthquake and fire devastated Chinatown, developers schemed to relocate Chinatown residents left homeless to less-desirable real estate outside the city. But representatives from the Chinese consulate and several gun-toting merchants marched back to Waverly Place, holding temple services amid the rubble at still-smoldering altars. The alley is the namesake of the main character in Amy Tan's bestselling *The Joy Luck Club*.

» **Spofford Alley** (🚌1, 15, 30, 45) Sun Yat-sen plotted the overthrow of China's last emperor at No 36, and the 1920s brought bootleggers' gun battles to this alley – but Spofford has mellowed with age. In the evenings you'll hear shuffling mahjong tiles and *erhu* (two-stringed Chinese fiddle) players warming up at local senior centers.

» **Ross Alley** (🚌1, 30, 45) Alternately known as Manila, Spanish and Mexico St after the working girls who once worked this block, mural-lined Ross Alley is occasionally pimped out for Hollywood productions, including *Karate Kid II* and *Indiana Jones and the Temple of Doom*. Duck into the alley's **Golden Gate Fortune Cookie Factory** (56 Ross Alley; admission free; ⊘8am-7pm) for custom cookies hot off the press (50¢ each), and write your own fortune.

Coit Tower
Historic Building

(☏415-362-0808; http://sfrecpark.org/destination/telegraph-hill-pioneer-park/coit-tower; Telegraph Hill Blvd; elevator entry (nonresident) adult/child $7/5; ⊘10am-5:30pm Mar-Sep, 9am-4:30pm Oct-Feb; 🚌39) Adding an exclamation mark to San Francisco's landscape, Coit Tower offers views worth shouting about – especially after you climb the giddy, steep Filbert St or Greenwich St steps to the top of Telegraph Hill. This 210ft, peculiar projectile is a monument to San Francisco firefighters financed by eccentric heiress Lillie Hitchcock Coit. Lillie could drink, smoke and play cards as well as any off-duty firefighter, rarely missed a fire or a firefighter's funeral, and even had the firehouse emblem embroidered on her bedsheets.

Asian Art Museum
Museum

(☏415-581-3500; www.asianart.org; 200 Larkin St; adult/student/child $12/8/free, 1st Sun of month free; ⊘10am-5pm Tue-Sun, to 9pm Thu; ♿; Ⓜ Civic Center, Ⓑ Civic Center) Imaginations race from ancient Persian miniatures to cutting-edge Japanese architecture through three floors spanning 6000 years of Asian arts. Besides the largest Asian art collection outside Asia – 18,000 works – the museum offers excellent programs for all ages, from shadow-puppet shows and yoga for kids to weeknight Artist's Drawing Club mixers with crosscultural DJ mashups.

City Lights Bookstore
Building

(☏415-362-8193; www.citylights.com; 261 Columbus Ave; ⊘10am-midnight) When founder and Beat poet Lawrence Ferlinghetti and manager Shigeyoshi Murao defended their right to 'willfully and lewdly print' Allen Ginsberg's magnificent *Howl and Other Poems* in 1957, City Lights became a free-speech landmark. Celebrate your freedom to read freely in the designated Poet's Chair upstairs overlooking Jack Kerouac Alley, load up on 'zines on the mezzanine and entertain radical ideas downstairs in the Muckraking and Stolen Continents sections.

Exploratorium
Museum

(☏415-528-4444; www.exploratorium.edu; Pier 15; adult/child $25/19, Thu evening $15; ⊘10am-5pm Tue-Sun, over-18yr only Thu 6-10pm; ℗♿; ⒻF) Is there a science to skateboarding? Do toilets flush conterclockwise in Australia? Find out first-hand with 600-plus fascinating, freaky exhibits. In under an hour you can star in psychedelic fractal music videos, make art from bacteria, and grope your way in total darkness through the Tactile Dome. Founded in 1969 by atom-bomb physicist Frank Oppenheimer, the newly relocated, expanded Exploratorium shows how life is cooler than science fiction.

Musée Mécanique
Amusement Park

(☏415-346-2000; www.museemechanique.org; Pier 45, Shed A; ⊘10am-7pm Mon-Fri, to 8pm Sat & Sun;

Downtown San Francisco & SoMa

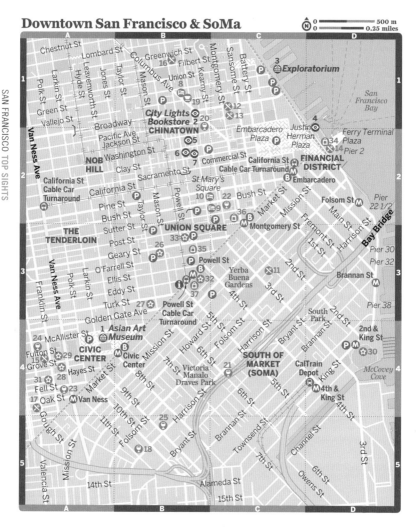

⚓ ; 🚋 47, 🚋 Powell-Mason, Powell-Hyde, Ⓜ F) Where else can you guillotine a man for a quarter? Creepy, 19th-century arcade games like the macabre French Execution compete for your spare change with the diabolical Ms Pac-Man.

Crissy Field   Park

(www.crissyfield.org; 1199 East Beach; 🚌 30, PresidioGo Shuttle) The Presidio's army airstrip has been stripped of asphalt and reinvented as a haven for coastal birds, kite-fliers and windsurfers enjoying sweeping views of Golden Gate Bridge.

Baker Beach   Beach

(☉ sunrise-sunset; 🚌 29, PresidiGo Shuttle) Unswimmable waters (except when the tide's coming in) but unbeatable views of the Golden Gate make this former Army beachhead SF's tanning location of choice, especially the clothing-optional north end – at least until the afternoon fog rolls in.

826 Valencia   Cultural Site

(📞 415-642-5905; www.826valencia.org; 826 Valencia St; ☉ noon-6pm; ⚓ ; 🚌 14, 33, 49, 🅑 16th St Mission, Ⓜ J) Avast, ye scurvy scalawags! If ye be shipwrecked without yer eye patch or Mc-

Downtown San Francisco & Soma

⊙ Top Sights
1 Asian Art Museum	A4
2 City Lights Bookstore	B1
3 Exploratorium	C1

⊙ Sights
4 Ferry Building	D1
5 Ross Alley	B2
6 Spofford Alley	B2
7 Waverly Place	B2

🛏 Sleeping
8 Hotel Bohème	B1
9 Hotel des Arts	C2
10 Orchard Garden Hotel	B2

✖ Eating
11 Benu	C3
12 Coi	C1
13 Cotogna	C1
14 Ferry Plaza Farmers Market	D2
Hog Island Oyster Company	see 4
15 Jardinière	A4
16 Liguria Bakery	B1
17 Rich Table	A4
Slanted Door	see 4

🍷 Drinking & Nightlife
18 Bar Agricole	B5
19 Caffe Trieste	B1
20 Comstock Saloon	B1
21 EndUp	C4
22 Rickhouse	C2
23 Rickshaw Stop	A4
24 Smuggler's Cove	A4
25 Stud	B5

✪ Entertainment
26 American Conservatory Theater	B3
27 Aunt Charlie's	B3
28 Davies Symphony Hall	A4
29 San Francisco Ballet	A4
30 San Francisco Giants	D4
San Francisco Opera	see 30
31 SFJAZZ Center	A4
32 Sisters of Perpetual Indulgence	B3
33 TIX Bay Area	B3

🛍 Shopping
34 Heath Ceramics	D2
35 Macy's	B3
36 Under One Roof	C2
37 Westfield San Francisco Centre	B3

Sweeney's literary anthology, lay down yer dubloons and claim yer booty at this here nonprofit Pirate Store. Below decks, kids be writing tall tales for dark nights asea, and ye can study making video games and magazines and suchlike, if that be yer dastardly inclination...arrr!

☞ Tours

Precita Eyes Mission Mural Tours   Tour

(☑ 415-285-2287; www.precitaeyes.org; adult $15-20, child $3; ☺ see website calendar for tour dates; ♿) Muralists lead two-hour tours on foot or bike covering 60 to 70 murals in a six- to 10-block radius of mural-bedecked Balmy Alley; proceeds fund mural upkeep at this community arts nonprofit.

Chinatown Alleyway Tours   Tour

(☑ 415-984-1478; www.chinatownalleywaytours.org; adult/student $18/12; ☺ 11am Sat; ♿; ☐ 8X, 8AX, 8BX) Neighborhood teens lead two-hour community nonprofit tours for up-close-and-personal peeks into Chinatown's past (weather permitting). Book five days ahead or pay double for Saturday walk-ins; cash only.

🎊 Festivals & Events

February

Lunar New Year   Cultural

(www.chineseparade.com) Firecrackers, legions of tiny-tot martial artists and a 200ft dancing dragon make this parade the highlight of San Francisco winters.

April & May

SF International Film Festival   Film

(www.sffs.org) Stars align and directors launch premieres each April at the nation's oldest film festival.

Bay to Breakers   Sport

(www.baytobreakers.com; race registration $58-89.50) Run costumed from Embarcadero to Ocean Beach (7.5 miles) on the third Sunday in May, while joggers dressed as salmon run upstream.

June

SF Pride Celebration   Cultural

A day isn't enough to do SF proud: June begins with International LGBT Film Festival

Alcatraz

Book a ferry from Pier 33 and ride 1.5 miles across the bay to explore America's most notorious former prison. The trip itself is worth the money, providing stunning views of the city skyline. Once you've landed at the **Ferry Dock & Pier ❶**, you begin the 580-yard walk to the top of the island and prison; if you're out of shape, there's a twice-hourly tram.

As you climb toward the **Guardhouse ❷**, notice the island's steep slope; before it was a prison, Alcatraz was a fort. In the 1850s, the military quarried the rocky shores into near-vertical cliffs. Ships could then only dock at a single port, separated from the main buildings by a sally port (a drawbridge and moat in what became the guardhouse). Inside, peer through floor grates to see Alcatraz' original prison.

Volunteers tend the brilliant **Officer's Row Gardens ❸** – an orderly counterpoint to the overgrown rose bushes surrounding the burned-out shell of the **Warden's House ❹**. At the top of the hill, by the front door of the **Main Cellhouse ❺**, beauty shots unfurl all around, including a **view of the Golden Gate Bridge ❻**. Above the main door of the administration building, notice the **historic signs & graffiti ❼**, before you step inside the dank, cold prison to find the **Frank Morris cell ❽**, former home to Alcatraz' most notorious jail-breaker.

TOP TIPS

» Book at least two weeks prior for self-guided daytime visits, longer for ranger-led night tours. For info on garden tours, see www.alcatraz gardens.org.

» Be prepared to hike; a steep path ascends from the ferry landing to the cell block. Most people spend two to three hours on the island. You need only reserve for the outbound ferry; take any ferry back.

» There's no food (just water) but you can bring your own; picnicking is allowed at the ferry dock only. Dress in layers as the weather changes fast and it's usually windy.

JOHN A VLAHIDES ©

Historic Signs & Graffiti
During their 1969–71 occupation, Native Americans graffitied the water tower: 'Home of the Free Indian Land.' Above the cellhouse door, examine the eagle-and-flag crest to see how the red-and-white stripes were changed to spell 'Free.'

Warden's House
Fires destroyed the warden's house and other structures during the Indian Occupation. The government blamed the Native Americans; the Native Americans blamed agents provocateurs acting on behalf of the Nixon Administration to undermine public sympathy.

Parade Grounds

DAVID CLAPP / GETTY IMAGES ©

Ferry Dock & Pier
A giant wall map helps you get your bearings. Inside nearby Bldg 64, short films and exhibits provide historical perspective on the prison and details about the Indian Occupation.

View of Golden Gate Bridge
The Golden Gate Bridge stretches wide on the horizon. Best views are from atop the island at Eagle Plaza, near the cellhouse entrance, and at water level along the Agave Trail (September to January only).

Main Cellhouse
During the mid-20th century, the maximum-security prison housed the day's most notorious troublemakers, including Al Capone and Robert Stroud, the 'Birdman of Alcatraz' (who actually conducted his ornithology studies at Leavenworth).

Power House

Recreation Yard

Water Tower

Officers' Club

Frank Morris Cell
Peer into cell 138 on B-Block to see a re-creation of the dummy's head that Frank Morris left in his bed as a decoy to aid his notorious – and successful – 1962 escape from Alcatraz.

Lighthouse

Guard Tower

Guardhouse
Alcatraz' oldest building dates to 1857 and retains remnants of the original drawbridge and moat. During the Civil War the basement was transformed into a military dungeon – the genesis of Alcatraz as prison.

Officer's Row Gardens
In the 19th century soldiers imported topsoil to beautify the island with gardens. Well-trusted prisoners later gardened – Elliott Michener said it kept him sane. Historians, ornithologists and archaeologists choose today's plants.

MISSION MURALS

Inspired by Diego Rivera's San Francisco Works Progress Administration (WPA) murals and outraged by US foreign policy in Central America, Mission *muralistas* set out in the 1970s to transform the political landscape, one alley at a time. Today, 400-plus murals line Mission streets, including:

Balmy Alley (☑415-285-2277; www.precitaeyes.org; btwn 24th & 25th Sts; ☐10, 12, 27, 33, 48, Ⓑ24th St Mission) Between Treat Ave and Harrison St, murals spanning 35 years transform garage doors into artistic and political statements, from an early memorial for El Salvador activist Archbishop Òscar Romero to a homage to the golden age of Mexican cinema.

Clarion Alley (btwn 17th & 18th Sts, off Valencia St; ☐14, 22, 33, Ⓑ16th St Mission, ⓂJ) Only the strongest street art survives in Clarion, where lesser works are peed on or painted over. Very few pieces survive for years, such as Megan Wilson's daisy-covered *Capitalism Is Over (If You Want It)* or Jet Martinez' view of Clarion Alley within a man standing in a forest.

Women's Building (3543 18th St; ⚙; Ⓜ18th St, Ⓑ16th St Mission) San Francisco's biggest mural is the 1994 *MaestraPeace*, a show of female strength painted by 90 *muralistas* that hugs the Women's Building. Featured icons range from ancient Mayan and Chinese goddesses to modern trailblazers, including Nobel Prize–winner Rigoberta Menchu, poet Audre Lorde and artist Georgia O'Keeffe.

(www.frameline.org; ☉mid-Jun) and goes out in style the last weekend with Pink Saturday's **Dyke March** (www.dykemarch.org) and **Pride Parade** (www.sfpride.org).

August & September

Outside Lands
Music

(www.sfoutsidelands.com/; 1-/3-day $115/375) Three days of major acts – such as Kanye West, Macklemore, The Killers, The Flaming Lips – and outlandish debauchery at Wine Land, Beer Lands and Taste of the Bay.

Folsom Street Fair
Street Fair

(www.folsomstreetfair.com) Work that leather look and enjoy public spankings for local charities the last weekend of September.

October & November

Litquake
Literature

(www.litquake.org) Score signed books and grab drinks with authors in October.

Hardly Strictly Bluegrass
Music

(www.strictlybluegrass.com) Three days of free Golden Gate Park concerts and headliners ranging from Elvis Costello to Gillian Welch; early October.

Día de los Muertos
Festival

(Day of the Dead; www.dayofthedeadsf.org) Party to wake the dead with a spooky costume parade, sugar skulls and fabulous altars in the Mission on November 2.

🛏 Sleeping

Hotel des Arts
Hotel $

(☑415-956-3232, 800-956-4322; www.sfhoteldesarts. com; 447 Bush St; r with bath $129-199, without bath $99; ☎; ⓂMontgomery, ⒷMontgomery) A budget hotel for art freaks, with jaw-dropping murals by underground artists – it's like sleeping inside a painting. Rooms with private bath require seven-night stays. Bring earplugs.

HI San Francisco
Fisherman's Wharf
Hostel $

(☑415-771-7277; www.sfhostels.com; Bldg 240, Fort Mason; dm incl breakfast $30-42, r $75-109; Ⓟ@☎; ☐28, 30, 47, 49) A former army hospital building offers bargain-priced private rooms and dorms (some co-ed) with four to 22 beds and a huge kitchen. No curfew, but no heat during the day – bring warm clothes. Limited free parking.

San Remo Hotel
Hotel $$

(☎415-776-8688, 800-352-7366; www.sanremo hotel.com; 2237 Mason St; r with shared bath $99-139; @🛜🐾; 🚇30, 47, 🚋Powell-Mason) One of the city's best-value stays, this 1906 inn is an old-fashioned charmer with antique furnishings. Bargain rooms have windows facing the corridor; family suites accommodate up to five. No elevator.

Inn San Francisco
B&B $$

(☎800-359-0913, 415-641-0188; www.innsf.com; 943 S Van Ness Ave; r incl breakfast $185-310, with shared bath $135-200; P@🛜; 🚇14, 49) 🍃 An impeccably maintained 1872 Italianate-Victorian mansion, this inn has period antiques, fresh-cut flowers, and fluffy featherbeds; some rooms have Jacuzzi tubs. There's also a free-standing garden cottage that sleeps up to six. Outside there's an English garden and redwood hot tub. Limited parking: reserve ahead.

Orchard Garden Hotel
Boutique Hotel $$$

(☎415-399-9807, 888-717-2881; www.theorchard gardenhotel.com; 466 Bush St; r $295-370; ❄@🛜; 🚇2, 3, 30, 45, Ⓑ Montgomery) 🍃 San Francisco's first all-green-practices hotel features sustainable wood furnishings, chemical-free cleaning products, and a sunny rooftop terrace. Luxe touches include down pillows and Egyptian-cotton sheets in soothingly quiet rooms.

Hotel Bohème
Boutique Hotel $$$

(☎415-433-9111; www.hotelboheme.com; 444 Columbus Ave; r $214-275; @🛜; 🚇10, 12, 30, 41, 45) A love letter to the Beat era, with vintage photos, parasol lights and moody 1950s color schemes. Rooms are smallish and some face noisy Columbus Ave – but the vibrant North Beach neighborhood scene could inspire your next novel.

Argonaut Hotel
Boutique Hotel $$$

(☎415-563-0800, 800-790-1415; www. argonauthotel.com; 495 Jefferson St; r $389-449, with view $489-529; ❄🛜🐾; 🚇19, 47, 49, 🚋Powell-Hyde) 🍃 Built as a cannery in 1908, Fisherman's Wharf's best inn has century-old wooden beams, exposed brick walls and an over-the-top nautical theme that includes porthole-shaped mirrors. Ultra-comfy beds and iPod docks are standard, though some rooms are small and dark – pay extra for mesmerising bay views.

Hotel Drisco
Boutique Hotel $$$

(☎415-346-2880, 800-634-7277; www.hoteldrisco. com; 2901 Pacific Ave; r incl breakfast $375-425; @🛜; 🚇3, 24) A stately apartment-hotel tucked between Pacific Heights mansions, with elegant architecture, attentive service and understated-chic room decor. At this lofty ridgeline location, spring for city-view rooms and taxis.

Telegraph Hill

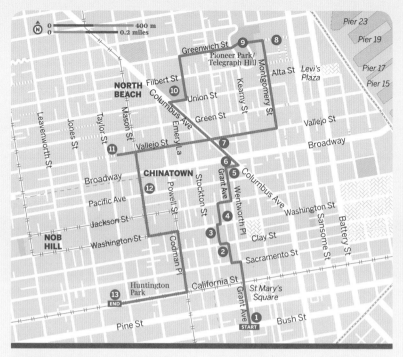

City Walk
San Francisco Hilltops

START DRAGON GATE
FINISH GRACE CATHEDRAL
LENGTH 2.3 MILES; 2½ HOURS

Conquer San Francisco's three most famous hills – Telegraph, Russian and Nob – for views that are pure poetry.

Enter Chinatown's ❶ **Dragon Gate** and walk up dragon-lantern-lined Grant Ave to Sacramento St. Turn left half a block up, then right onto ❷ **Waverly Place** (p55), where prayer flags grace painted temple balconies. At Clay St, jog left and right again onto ❸ **Spofford Alley** (p55), where Sun Yat-sen plotted revolution. At the end of the block on Washington, take a right and an immediate left onto mural-lined ❹ **Ross Alley** (p55), once San Francisco's bordello byway.

Turn right down Jackson, left on Grant, then turn right onto ❺ **Jack Kerouac Alley**, where the pavement echoes Kerouac's ode to San Francisco: 'The air was soft, the stars so fine, and the promise of every cobbled alley so great...' Ahead is literary landmark ❻ **City**

Lights (p55), where you'll pause to read a poem upstairs in the designated Poet's Chair.

Head left up Columbus and veer right up Vallejo to fuel up with an espresso at ❼ **Caffe Trieste** (p65), where Francis Ford Coppola drafted his script for *The Godfather*. Continue up Vallejo and scale the steps to Montgomery St. Go left three blocks, and turn left onto cottage-lined ❽ **Greenwich Street Steps** to summit Telegraph Hill. Inside ❾ **Coit Tower** (p54), enjoy 1934 city views in newly restored murals downstairs and panoramic Bay views up top.

Head downhill, past wild parrots and tai-chi masters at ❿ **Washington Square**. Turn left on Columbus, right on Vallejo, and up three blocks to take another picturesque stairway path to flower-lined ⓫ **Ina Coolbrith Park**. Any breath you have left will be taken away by sweeping views to Alcatraz. Summit your last hill of the day the easy way: catch the ⓬ **Powell-Mason cable car** up Nob Hill to walk the meditation labyrinth at ⓭ **Grace Cathedral**.

✕ Eating

Liguria Bakery Bakery $
(☑415-421-3786; 1700 Stockton St; focaccia $4-5; ⏱8am-1pm Tue-Fri, from 7am Sat; ✎🚻; 🚍8X, 30, 39, 41, 45, 🚋Powell-Mason) Bleary-eyed art students and Italian grandmothers line up by 8am for cinnamon-raisin focaccia hot from the 100-year-old oven, leaving 9am dawdlers a choice of tomato or classic rosemary. Take yours in wax paper or boxed for picnics; cash only.

La Taqueria Mexican $
(☑415-285-7117; 2889 Mission St; burritos $6-8; ⏱11am-9pm Mon-Sat, to 8pm Sun; 🚻; 🚍12, 14, 48, 49, Ⓑ24th St Mission) SF's definitive burrito has no debatable saffron rice, spinach tortilla or mango salsa – just perfectly grilled meats, slow-cooked beans and classic tomatillo or mesquite salsa wrapped in flour tortillas.

Cotogna Italian $$
(☑415-775-8508; www.cotognasf.com; 490 Pacific Ave; mains $17-29; ⏱11:30am-11pm Mon-Thu, 11:30am-midnight Fri & Sat, 5-9:30pm Sun; ✎; 🚍10, 12) Rustic Italian pastas, wood-fired pizzas and rotisserie meats spiked with rooftop-grown herbs show chef Michael Tusk's finesse with well-chosen, balanced ingredients. Book ahead or plan a late lunch.

Greens Vegetarian, Californian $$
(☑415-771-6222; www.greensrestaurant.com; Bldg A, Fort Mason Center, cnr Marina Blvd & Laguna St; lunch $15-18, dinner $18-25; ⏱11:45am-2:30pm & 5:30-9pm Tue-Fri, from 11am Sat, 10:30am-2pm & 5:30-9pm Sun, 5:30-9pm Mon; ✎🚻; 🚍28) 🏳 Career carnivores won't realize there's zero meat in hearty roasted-eggplant panini and black-bean chili with crème fraîche and pickled jalapeños – they're packed with flavor-bursting ingredients grown on a Zen farm in Marin. Make reservations on weekends, or get take-out to enjoy on a wharf-side bench.

Ichi Sushi Sushi $$
(☑415-525-4750; www.ichisushi.com; 3282 Mission St; sushi $4-8; ⏱5:30-10pm Mon-Thu, to 11pm Fri & Sat; 🚍14, 49, Ⓑ24th St Mission, Ⓜ J) Ichi Sushi is a sharp cut above other fish joints. Silky, sustainably sourced fish is sliced with a jeweler's precision, balanced atop well-packed rice, and topped with powerfully tangy dabs of gelled yuzu and microscopically diced chili daikon that make soy sauce unthinkable.

Namu Gaji Korean, Californian $$
(☑415-431-6268; www.namusf.com; 499 Dolores St; small plates $10-21; ⏱11:30am-4pm Wed-Fri, from 10:30am Sat & Sun, 5-10pm Tue-Thu & Sun, 5-11pm Fri & Sat; 🚍22, 33, Ⓜ, Ⓑ16th St Mission) 🏳 SF's culinary advantages are showcased in Namu's Korean-inspired soul food. Menu standouts include ultra-savory shiitake mushroom dumplings, meltingly tender marinated beef tongue, and a sizzling stone pot of rice with organic vegetables, grass-fed steak and a Sonoma farm egg.

Outerlands Californian $$
(☑415-661-6140; www.outerlandssf.com; 4001 Judah St; sandwiches & small plates $7-14, mains $18-22; ⏱10am-3pm Tue-Fri, from 9am Sat & Sun, 5:30-10pm Tue-Sun; 🚻; 🚍18, Ⓜ N) 🏳 When windy Ocean Beach leaves you feeling shipwrecked, drift into this beach-shack bistro for organic, seed-to-table California comfort food. Brunch demands Dutch pancakes in iron skillets with housemade ricotta, and lunch brings grilled artisan-cheese combos with farm-inspired soup. Reserve ahead or enjoy wine while you wait.

Coi Californian $$$
(☑415-393-9000; www.coirestaurant.com; 373 Broadway; set menu $195; ⏱5:30-10pm Tue-Sat; 🚍8X, 30, 41, 45, 🚋Powell-Mason) 🏳 Chef Daniel Patterson's restlessly imaginative eight-course tasting menu is like licking California's coastline: rooftop-raised pansies grace Sonoma duck's tongue, and wild-caught abalone surfaces in pea-shoot tidepools. Settle in among the shaggy cushions and spot-lit stoneware to enjoy only-in-California wine pairings ($115; generous enough for two).

Gary Danko Californian $$$
(☑415-749-2060; www.garydanko.com; 800 North Point St; 3-/5-course menu $76/111; ⏱5:30-10pm; 🚍19, 30, 47, 🚋Powell-Hyde) The true test of SF romance is whether you're willing to share Gary Danko's crèmes brûlée trio. Smoked-glass windows prevent passersby from tripping over their tongues at roast lobster with trumpet mushrooms, duck breast with rhubarb compote, and the lavish cheese cart. Reservations required.

Benu Californian, Fusion $$$
(☑415-685-4860; www.benusf.com; 22 Hawthorne St; tasting menu $195; ⏱5:30-8:30pm Tue-Sat; 🚍10, 12, 14, 30, 45) SF has refined fusion cuisine over 150 years, but no one rocks it quite like chef/owner Corey Lee (formerly

THE FERRY BUILDING

San Francisco's monument to food, the Ferry Building (☑415-983-8000; www.ferrybuildingmarketplace.com; Market St & the Embarcadero; ◷10am-6pm Mon-Fri, 9am-6pm Sat, 11am-5pm Sun; Ⓟ🚻; Ⓜ Embarcadero, Ⓑ Embarcadero) still doubles as a trans-bay transit hub – but with dining options like these, you may never leave.

Ferry Plaza Farmers Market (☑415-291-3276; www.cuesa.org; Market St & the Embarcadero; ◷10am-2pm Tue & Thu, 8am-2pm Sat; Ⓜ Embarcadero, Ⓑ Embarcadero) Star chefs troll farmers-market stalls for rare heirloom varietals, foodie babies blissfully teethe on organic apricots, and organic tamale trucks have rock-star fan bases. Pass time in line exchanging recipe tips, then haul your picnic to Pier 2.

Slanted Door (☑415-861-8032; www.slanteddoor.com; 1 Ferry Bldg; lunch $16-36, dinner $18-45; ◷11am-4:30pm & 5:30-10pm Mon-Sat, 11:30am-4:30pm & 5:30-10pm Sun; Ⓜ Embarcadero, Ⓑ Embarcadero) Charles Phan earns his 2014 James Beard Outstanding Chef title with California-fresh, Vietnamese-inspired fare that rivals the sparkling Bay views – especially five-spice duck with figs. Reserve ahead or hit the takeout window.

Hog Island Oyster Company (☑415-391-7117; www.hogislandoysters.com; 1 Ferry Bldg; 4 oysters $13; ◷11:30am-9pm Mon-Thu, to 10pm Fri, 11am-10pm Sat, 11am-9pm Sun; Ⓜ Embarcadero, Ⓑ Embarcadero) 🍴 Slurp sustainably farmed Tomales Bay oysters as you please: drizzled with tangy caper buerre blanc, spiked with bacon and paprika, or au naturel with Sonoma bubbly.

of Napa's French Laundry), who remixes local, sustainable, fine-dining staples and Pacific Rim flavors with a SoMa DJ's finesse. Dungeness crab and truffle bring such outsize flavor to his faux-shark's-fin soup, you'll swear there's Jaws in there.

Frances
Californian $$$

(☑415-621-3870; www.frances-sf.com; 3870 17th St; mains $20-27; ◷5-10pm Sun-Thu, to 10:30pm Fri & Sat; Ⓜ Castro) Chef/owner Melissa Perello ditched downtown fine dining to start this bistro showcasing bright, seasonal flavors and luxurious textures: cloudlike sheep's-milk ricotta gnocchi with crunchy broccolini, grilled calamari with preserved Meyer lemon, and artisan wine served by the ounce, directly from Wine Country.

Rich Table
Californian $$$

(☑415-355-9085; http://richtablesf.com; 199 Gough St; meals $17-30; ◷5:30-10pm Sun-Thu, to 10:30pm Fri & Sat; 🚌5, 6, 21, 47, 49, 71, Ⓜ Van Ness) 🍴 Licking plates is the obvious move after finishing chilled apricot soup with pancetta or rabbit cannelloni with nasturtium cream. Married co-chefs/co-owners Sarah and Evan Rich invent playful, exquisite Californian food like the Dirty Hippie: silky goat-buttermilk panna-cotta topped with sunflower seeds and hemp. Book two to four weeks ahead (call the restaurant directly) or arrive early for bar seating.

Jardinière
Californian $$$

(☑415-861-5555; www.jardiniere.com; 300 Grove St; mains $18-32; ◷5-10:30pm Tue-Sat, to 10pm Sun & Mon; 🚌5, 21, 47, 49, Ⓜ Van Ness) 🍴 Iron Chef, Top Chef Master and James Beard Award-winner Traci Des Jardins champions sustainable, salacious California cuisine. She lavishes housemade tagliatelle with bone marrow and tops velvety scallops with satiny sea urchin. Go Mondays, when $55 scores three decadent courses with wine pairings.

Aziza
Moroccan, Californian $$$

(☑415-752-2222; www.aziza-sf.com; 5800 Geary Blvd; mains $19-29; ◷5:30-10:30pm Wed-Mon; 🚌1, 29, 31, 38) Iron Chef champ Mourad Lahlou's inspiration is Moroccan and his ingredients organic Californian, but the flavors are out of this world: Sonoma duck confit and caramelized onion fill flaky pastry basteeya, and slow-cooked Marin lamb tops saffron-infused barley. Pastry chef Melissa Chou's apricot bavarian is a goodnight kiss.

🍷 Drinking & Nightlife

Rickhouse
Bar

(☑415-398-2827; www.rickhousebar.com; 246 Kearny St; ◷5pm-2am Mon, 3pm-2am Tue-Fri, 6pm-2am Sat; Ⓜ Montgomery, Ⓑ Montgomery)

Like a shotgun shack plunked downtown, Rickhouse is lined with bourbon casks and shelving from an Ozark Mountains nunnery that once secretly brewed hooch. The emphasis is on rare bourbon, but groups guzzle authentic Pisco Punch by the garage-sale punchbowl.

Caffe Trieste   Cafe

(415-392-6739; www.caffetrieste.com; 601 Vallejo St; 6:30am-11pm Sun-Thu, to midnight Fri & Sat; ; 8X, 10, 12, 30, 41, 45) Poetry on bathroom walls, opera on the jukebox, live accordion jams weekly and sightings of Beat poet laureate Lawrence Ferlinghetti: Trieste has been a North Beach landmark since the 1950s. Sip espresso under the Sicilian mural, where Francis Ford Coppola drafted *The Godfather*. Cash only.

Comstock Saloon   Bar

(415-617-0071;   www.comstocksaloon.com; 155 Columbus Ave; noon to 2am Mon-Fri, from 4pm Sat, 4pm-midnight Sun; 8X, 10, 12, 30, 45, Powell-Mason) Cocktails at this Victorian saloon remain period-perfect: Pisco Punch is made with pineapple gum and martini-precursor Martinez features gin, vermouth, bitters and maraschino liqueur. Call ahead for booths or tufted-velvet parlor seating and to get dates when ragtime-jazz bands play.

Bar Agricole   Bar

(415-355-9400; www.baragricole.com; 355 11th St; 6-10pm Tue-Thu & Sun, 5:30-11pm Fri & Sat; 9, 12, 27, 47) Drink your way to a history degree with these cocktails: Bellamy Scotch Sour with egg whites passes the test, but Tequila Fix with lime, pineapple gum and hellfire bitters earns honors. Don't miss the sea-urchin deviled eggs.

Smuggler's Cove   Bar

(415-869-1900; www.smugglerscovesf.com; 650 Gough St; 5pm-1:15am; 5, 21, 49, Van Ness) Yo-ho-ho and a bottle of rum...or perhaps a Dead Reckoning with bitters, Nicaraguan rum, tawny port and vanilla liqueur. Pirates are bedeviled by choice at this shipwreck tiki speakeasy – with 400 rums and 70 cocktails, you won't be dry-docked long.

Toronado   Pub

(415-863-2276; www.toronado.com; 547 Haight St; 11:30am-2am; 6, 22, 71, N) Glory hallelujah, beer lovers: your prayers are answered with 50-plus brews on tap and hundreds more bottled. Bring cash and pair seasonal ales with sausages from Rosamunde (415-437-6851; http://rosamundesausagegrill.com; 545 Haight St; sausages $6.50-7; 11:30am-10pm Sun-Wed, to 11pm Thu-Sat; 6, 22, 71, N) next door – it may get too loud to hear your date, but you'll hear angels sing.

Ferry Plaza Farmers Market

☆ Entertainment

At TIX Bay Area (www.tixbayarea.org), half-price tickets are sold on show day for cash only. For advance tickets to concerts and Broadway shows, check Ticketmaster (www.ticketmaster.com) and SHN (www.shnsf.com).

Castro Theatre   Cinema

See page 19

SFJAZZ Center   Jazz

(☏866-920-5299; www.sfjazz.org; 201 Franklin St; ☺showtimes vary; ▣5, 7, 21, Ⓜ Van Ness) America's newest, largest jazz center draws legendary artists-in-residence like Wynton Marsalis, Regina Carter and Tony Bennett (who left his heart here, after all) – but the real thrills are experimental performances, like pianist Jason Moran's jam session with SF skateboarders pounding a ramp inside the auditorium.

Upper-tier cheap seats are more like stools, but offer clear stage views and ledges for drinks.

The Chapel   Live Music

(☏415-551-5157; www.thechapelsf.com; 777 Valencia St; tickets $15-22; ▣14, 33, Ⓜ J, Ⓑ 16th St Mission) Musical prayers are answered in a 1914 California Craftsman landmark with heavenly acoustics. The 40ft roof is raised by shows like Preservation Hall Jazz Band jams with Nick Lowe, Polyphonic Spree's full-choir ruckus and Radiohead's *OK Computer* lip-synched by an all-star drag revue. Many shows are all-ages, except when comedians like W Kamau Bell test edgy material.

The Fillmore   Concert Venue

(☏415-346-3000; www.thefillmore.com; 1805 Geary Blvd; tickets from $20; ☺shows nightly) Hendrix, Zeppelin, Janis all played the Fillmore. The

GAY/LESBIAN/BI/TRANS SAN FRANCISCO

Singling out the best places to be queer in San Francisco is almost redundant. Though the Castro is a gay hub and the Mission is a magnet for lesbians, dancing queens and party bois head to SoMa for thump-thump clubs. Top GLBT venues include:

Stud (www.studsf.com; 399 9th St; admission $5-8; ☺noon-2am Tue, from 5pm Wed & Sat, 5pm-3am Thu & Fri, 5pm to midnight Sun; ▣12, 19, 27, 47) Rocking the gay scene since 1966, and branching out beyond leather daddies with rocker-grrrl Mondays, Tuesday drag variety shows, raunchy comedy/karaoke Wednesdays, Friday art-drag dance parties, and performance-art cabaret whenever hostess/DJ Anna Conda gets it together.

Lexington Club (☏415-863-2052; www.lexingtonclub.com; 3464 19th St; ☺5pm-2am Mon-Thu, from 3pm Fri-Sun; ▣14, 33, 49, Ⓑ 16th St Mission) Odds are eerily high you'll develop a crush on your ex-girlfriend's hot new girlfriend over strong drinks, pinball and tattoo comparisons; live dangerously at SF's most famous/notorious full-time lesbian bar.

Aunt Charlie's (☏415-441-2922; www.auntcharlieslounge.com; 133 Turk St; admission $2-5; ☺noon-2am Mon-Fri, from 10am Sat, 10am-midnight Sun; Ⓜ Powell, Ⓑ Powell) Total dive, with the city's best classic drag show Fridays and Saturdays at 10pm. Thursday nights, art-school boys freak for bathhouse disco at Tubesteak ($5).

Endup (☏415-646-0999; www.theendup.com; 401 6th St; admission $5-20; ☺10pm Thu-4am Fri, 11pm Fri-11am Sat, 10pm Sat-4am Mon, 10pm Mon-4am Tue; ▣12, 27, 47) Home of Sunday 'tea dances' since 1973, though technically the party starts Saturday, EndUp watching the sunrise Monday over the freeway on-ramp.

Rickshaw Stop (☏415-861-2011; www.rickshawstop.com; 155 Fell St; admission $5-35; ☺variable, check online; Ⓜ Van Ness) Freak beats keep sweaty 18-plus crowds up past their bedtimes at this all-ages, all-orientations, all-fabulous shoebox club; lesbian go-go and bhangra nights rule.

Sisters of Perpetual Indulgence (www.thesisters.org) For guerrilla antics and wild fundraisers, check the website of the self-described 'leading-edge order of queer nuns,' a charitable organization and San Francisco institution.

legendary venue that launched the psychedelic era has the posters to prove it upstairs, and hosts arena acts in a 1250-seat venue where you can squeeze in next to the stage.

American Conservatory Theater — Theater

(ACT; ☑ 415-749-2228; www.act-sf.org; 415 Geary St; ⊙ box office noon-6pm Mon, to curtain Tue-Sun; 🚇 38, 🚋 Powell-Mason, Powell-Hyde) Breakthrough shows destined for Broadway premiere at ACT's Geary Theater, including Tony Kushner's *Angels in America* and Robert Wilson's *Black Rider*, with a libretto by William S Burroughs and music by Tom Waits.

Davies Symphony Hall — Classical Music

(☑ rush tickets 415-503-5577, 415-864-6000; www.sfsymphony.org; 201 Van Ness Ave; Ⓜ Van Ness, Ⓑ Civic Center) SF Symphony has racked up nine Grammys, and you can see why: conductor Michael Tilson Thomas keeps the audience rapt through Beethoven, Mahler, even Metallica. The season runs September to July; call the rush-ticket hotline for $20 next-day tickets, and don't miss free pre-show talks.

San Francisco Opera — Opera

(☑ 415-864-3330; www.sfopera.com; War Memorial Opera House, 301 Van Ness Ave; tickets $10-350; Ⓑ Civic Center, Ⓜ Van Ness) SF Opera rivals New York's Met with original operas like Stephen King's *Dolores Claiborne* and Verdi and Puccini revivals by acclaimed Tuscan director Nicola Luisotti. Book ahead, or score $10 same-day, standing-room tickets at 10am and two hours before curtain.

ODC Theater — Dance

(☑ 415-863-9834; www.odctheater.org; 3153 17th St; ⊙ box office noon-3pm Mon-Fri) For 40 years, ODC has redefined dance with risky, raw performances September through December – plus year-round guest performers and 200 dance classes a week.

San Francisco Ballet — Dance

(☑ 415-861-5600, tickets 415-865-2000; www.sfballet.org; War Memorial Opera House, 301 Van Ness Ave; tickets $10-120; Ⓜ Van Ness, Ⓑ Civic Center) SF Ballet performs 100 gloriously staged shows annually at the War Memorial Opera House January to May; check website for dates and ticket deals.

Roxie Cinema — Cinema

(☑ 415-863-1087; www.roxie.com; 3117 16th St; regular screening/matinee $10/7; 🚇 14, 22, 33, 49, Ⓑ 16th St Mission) A little neighborhood nonprofit cinema with major international clout for indie premieres, controversial films and documentaries banned elsewhere. No ads, plus personal introductions to every film.

San Francisco Giants — Baseball

(☑ 415-972-2000; www.sfgiants.com; AT&T Park, 24 Willie Mays Plaza; tickets $5-135) Watch and learn how the World Series is won.

🛍 Shopping

San Francisco has big department stores and name-brand boutiques around Union Sq, including Macy's (www.macys.com; 170 O'Farrell St; ⊙ 10am-9pm Mon-Sat, 11am-7pm Sun; 🚋 Powell-Mason, Powell-Hyde, Ⓜ Powell, Ⓑ Powell) and Westfield San Francisco Centre (www.westfield.com/sanfrancisco; 865 Market St; ⊙ 10am-8:30pm Mon-Sat, to 7pm Sun; ♿; 🚋 Powell-Mason, Powell-Hyde, Ⓜ Powell, Ⓑ Powell) – but only-in-SF stores are found in the Haight, Castro, Mission and Hayes Valley.

Under One Roof — Gifts

(☑ 415-503-2300; www.underoneroof.org; Crocker Galleria, 50 Post St; ⊙ 10am-6pm Mon-Fri) AIDS service organizations receive 100% of the proceeds from goods donated by local designers and retailers, so show volunteer salespeople some love.

Gravel & Gold — Housewares, Gifts

(☑ 415-552-0112; www.gravelandgold.com; 3266 21st St; ⊙ noon-7pm Mon-Sat, to 5pm Sun; Ⓜ 24th St Mission, Ⓑ 24th St Mission) Get back to the land and in touch with California roots with Gravel & Gold's trippy silkscreened totes, hippie homesteader smock-dresses, 1960s Osborne/Woods ecology posters, and rare books on '70s beach-shack architecture.

Park Life — Art, Gifts

(☑ 415-386-7275; www.parklifestore.com; 220 Clement St; ⊙ noon-8pm Mon-Thu, from 11am Fri & Sat, 11am-7pm Sun; 🚇 1, 2, 33, 38, 44) Design store, indie publisher and art gallery in one. Park Life presents are too good to wait for birthdays, including Golden State pendants, Sean O'Dell utopia catalogs, and Ian Johnson's portrait of John Coltrane radiating rainbow vibes.

Heath Ceramics — Housewares

(☑ 415-399-9284; www.heathceramics.com; 1 Ferry Bldg; ⊙ 10am-7pm Mon-Fri, 8am-6pm Sat, 11am-5pm Sun; Ⓜ Embarcadero, Ⓑ Embarcadero) No SF tablescape is complete without handmade modern Heath stoneware, thrown by pot-

Castro Theatre (p19)

ters in Heath's Sausalito studio since 1948. Pieces are priced for fine dining except studio seconds, sold on weekends.

Betabrand Clothing

(☑800-694-9491; www.betabrand.com; 780 Valencia St; ⊗11am-7pm Mon-Fri, to 8pm Sat, noon-6pm Sun; 📺14, 22, 33, 49, Ⓑ16th St Mission) Experimental designs are put to online votes and winners produced in limited editions. Recent designs include lunch-meat-patterned socks, reversible smoking jackets, and bike-to-work pants with reflective-strip cuffs.

ℹ️ Information

DANGERS & ANNOYANCES

Keep your city smarts and wits sharp, especially at night in SoMa, the Mission and the Haight. Unless you know where you're going, avoid the seedy, depressing Tenderloin (bordered east–west by Powell and Polk Sts and north–south by O'Farrell and Market Sts), Skid Row (6th St between Market and Folsom Sts) and Bayview–Hunters Point. Panhandlers and homeless people are part of San Francisco's community. People will probably ask you for spare change, but donations to local nonprofits stretch further. Don't engage with panhandlers at night or around ATMs. A simple 'I'm sorry,' is a polite response.

EMERGENCY & MEDICAL SERVICES

Haight Ashbury Free Clinic (☑415-762-3700; www.healthright360.org; 558 Clayton St; ⊗by appointment; 📺6, 33, 37, 43, 71, ⓂN) Provides substance abuse and mental health services by appointment.

San Francisco General Hospital (☑emergency 415-206-8111, main hospital 415-206-8000; www.sfdph.org; 1001 Potrero Ave; ⊗24hr; 📺9, 10, 33, 48) Provides care to uninsured patients; no documentation required.

Walgreens (☑415-861-3136; www.walgreens.com; 498 Castro St, cnr 18th St; ⊗24hr; 📺24, 33, 35, ⓂF, K, L, M) Pharmacy and over-the-counter meds; locations citywide (see website).

INTERNET ACCESS

SF has free wi-fi hot spots citywide – locate one nearby with www.openwifispots.com.

Apple Store (☑415-392-0202; www.apple.com/retail/sanfrancisco; 1 Stockton St; ⊗9am-9pm Mon-Sat, 10am-8pm Sun; 📶; ⓂPowell St) Free wi-fi and internet terminal usage.

San Francisco Main Library (☑415-871-4294; www.sfpl.org; 100 Larkin St; ⊗10am-6pm Mon & Sat, 9am-8pm Tue-Thu, noon-6pm Fri, noon-5pm Sun; 📶; ⓂCivic Center) Free 15-minute internet terminal usage; spotty wi-fi access.

TOURIST INFORMATION

California Welcome Center (☑415-981-1280; www.visitcwc.com; Pier 39, Bldg P, Suite 241b; ⊗9am-7pm)

San Francisco Visitor Information Center (☑415-391-2000, events hotline 415-391-2001; www.onlyinsanfrancisco.com; lower level, Hallidie Plaza, Market & Powell Sts; ⊗9am-5pm Mon-Fri, to 3pm Sat & Sun; 📺Powell-Mason, Powell-Hyde, ⓂPowell St, ⒷPowell St) Provides practical information and runs a 24-hour events hotline.

USEFUL WEBSITES

Craig's List (http://sfbay.craigslist.org) Events, activities, partners, freebies and dates.

Eater (http://sf.eater.com) Food and bars.

Flavorpill (www.flavorpill.com) Live music, lectures, art openings and movie premieres.

The Bold Italic (www.theboldstalic.com) SF trends, openings and opinions.

Urban Daddy (www.urbandaddy.com) Bars, shops, restaurants and events.

❶ Getting Around

For Bay Area transit options, departures and arrivals, check 🖉 511 or www.511.org.

BART

Bay Area Rapid Transit (www.bart.gov; one way \$8.25) links San Francisco International Airport (SFO), the Mission, downtown and the East Bay. Within SF, one-way fares start at \$1.75.

BICYCLE

Bicycling is safest in Golden Gate Park and along the waterfront; rentals are readily available.

CAR

Avoid driving in San Francisco: street parking is rare and meter readers ruthless. Convenient downtown parking lots are at 5th and Mission Sts, Union Sq, and Sutter and Stockton Sts. Daily rates run \$25 to \$50.

If your car is towed for parking violations, retrieve it from **Autoreturn** (🖉 415-865-8200; www.autoreturn.com; 450 7th St, SoMa; ☺ 24hr; Ⓜ 27, 42). Fines run to \$73, plus towing and storage (\$453.75 for the first four hours).

Members of **American Automobile Association** (AAA; 🖉 800-222-4357, 415-773-1900; www.aaa.com; 160 Sutter St; ☺ 8:30am-5:30pm Mon-Fri) can call anytime for emergency service.

MUNI

MUNI (Municipal Transit Agency; www.sfmuni.com) operates bus, streetcar and cable-car lines. The standard fare for buses or streetcars is \$2, and tickets are good for transfers for 90 minutes; hang onto your ticket to avoid a \$100 fine. The cable-car fare is \$6 per ride.

MUNI Passport (1-/3-/7-days \$14/22/28) allows unlimited travel on all MUNI transport, including cable cars; it's sold at San Francisco Visitor Information Center and many hotels.

Key routes include:

California cable car California St between Market St and Van Ness Ave

F Fisherman's Wharf to Castro

J Downtown to Mission

K, L, M Downtown to Castro

N Caltrain to Haight and Ocean Beach

Powell-Mason and **Powell-Hyde cable cars** Powell and Market Sts to Fisherman's Wharf

T Embarcadero to Caltrain

RIDESHARE & TAXI

SF-based rideshare companies including **Uber** (www.uber.com) and **Lyft** (www.lyft.com) offer rides from mostly non-professional drivers at set rates, starting around \$15 for in-city rides. Expect fast dispatch and fares charged to your account; sign-up and/or app download required.

San Francisco taxi fares run \$2.75 per mile, plus 10% tip (\$1 minimum); meters start at \$3.50. SF taxis have their own app to hail and pay cabs, downloadable at www.flywheel.com. Major cab companies include:

DeSoto Cab (🖉 415-970-1300; www.desotogo.com)

Green Cab (🖉 415-626-4733) Fuel-efficient hybrids; worker-owned collective.

Luxor (🖉 415-282-4141; www.luxorcab.com)

Yellow Cab (🖉 415-333-3333; www.yellowcabsf.com)

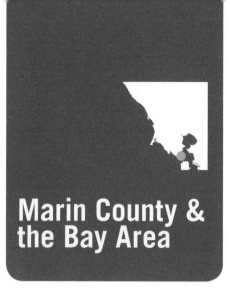

Marin County & the Bay Area

The region surrounding San Francisco encompasses a bonanza of natural vistas and wildlife.

Cross the Golden Gate Bridge to Marin and visit wizened ancient redwoods body-blocking the sun and herds of elegant tule elk prancing along the bluffs of Tomales Bay. Gray whales show some fluke off the cape of wind-scoured Point Reyes, and hawks surf the skies in the pristine hills of the Marin Headlands.

On the cutting edge of intellectual thought, Stanford University and the University of California at Berkeley draw academics and students from around the world. The city of Berkeley sparked the locavore food movement and continues to be on the forefront of environmental and left-leaning political causes. South of San Francisco, Hwy 1 traces miles of undeveloped coastline and sandy pocket beaches.

MARIN COUNTY

If there's a part of the Bay Area that consciously attempts to live up to the California dream, it's Marin County. Just across the Golden Gate Bridge from San Francisco, the region has a wealthy population that cultivates a seemingly laid-back lifestyle. Towns may look like idyllic rural hamlets, but the shops cater to cosmopolitan and expensive tastes. The 'common' folk here eat organic, vote Democrat and drive hybrids.

Geographically, Marin County is a near mirror image of San Francisco. It's a south-pointing peninsula that nearly touches the north-pointing tip of the city, and is surrounded by ocean and bay. But Marin is wilder, greener and more mountainous. Redwoods grow on the coast side of the hills, the surf crashes against cliffs, and hiking and cycling trails crisscross the blessed scenery of Point Reyes, Muir Woods and Mt Tamalpais. Nature is what makes Marin County such an excellent day trip or weekend escape from San Francisco.

❶ Information

The **Marin Convention & Visitors Bureau** (☏ 866-925-2060, 415-925-2060; www.visitmarin.org; 1 Mitchell Blvd, San Rafael; ⊘ 9am-5pm Mon-Fri) provides tourist information for the entire county.

❶ Getting There & Around

Busy Hwy 101 heads north from the Golden Gate Bridge ($7 toll when heading back into San Francisco), spearing through Marin's middle; quiet Hwy 1 winds its way along the sparsely populated coast. In San Rafael, Sir Francis Drake Blvd cuts across west Marin from Hwy 101 to the ocean.

Hwy 580 comes in from the East Bay over the Richmond–San Rafael bridge ($5 toll for westbound traffic) to meet Hwy 101 at Larkspur.

Marin Headlands

The headlands rise majestically out of the water at the north end of the Golden Gate

Bridge, their rugged beauty all the more striking given the fact that they're only a few miles from San Francisco's urban core. A few forts and bunkers are left over from a century of US military occupation – which is, ironically, the reason they are protected parklands today and free of development. It's no mystery why this is one of the Bay Area's most popular hiking and cycling destinations. As the trails wind through the headlands, they afford stunning views of the sea, the Golden Gate Bridge and San Francisco, leading to isolated beaches and secluded spots for picnics.

- - - - - - - - - - - - - - - - -

◉ Sights

After crossing the Golden Gate Bridge, exit immediately at Alexander Ave, then dip left under the highway and head out west for the expansive views and hiking trailheads. Conzelman Rd snakes up into the hills, where it eventually forks. Conzelman Rd continues west, becoming a steep, one-lane road as it descends to Point Bonita. From here it continues to Rodeo Beach and Fort Barry. McCullough Rd heads inland, joining Bunker Rd toward Rodeo Beach.

Hawk Hill   Hill
See page 18

Point Bonita Lighthouse   Lighthouse
(www.nps.gov/goga/pobo.htm; off Field Rd; ☺12:30-3:30pm Sat-Mon) **FREE** At the end of Conzelman Rd, this lighthouse is a breathtaking half-mile walk from a small parking area. From the tip of Point Bonita, you can see the distant Golden Gate Bridge and beyond it the San Francisco skyline. It's an uncommon vantage point of the bay-centric city, and harbor seals haul out nearby in season. To reserve a spot on one of the free monthly full-moon tours of the promontory, call ☐ 415-331-1540.

Nike Missile Site SF-88   Historic Site
(☐ 415-331-1453;   www.nps.gov/goga/nike-missile-site.htm; off Field Rd; ☺12:30pm-3:30pm Thu-Sat) **FREE** File past guard shacks with uniformed mannequins to witness the area's not-too-distant military history at this fascinating Cold War museum staffed by veterans. Watch them place a now-warhead-free missile into position, then ride a missile elevator to the cavernous underground silo to see the multikeyed launch controls that were thankfully never set in motion.

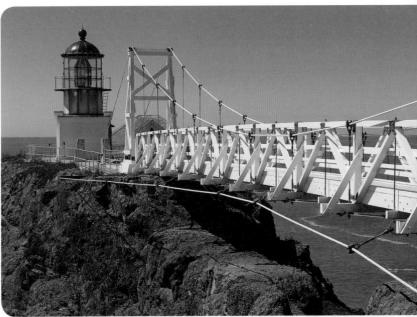

RICHARD CUMMINS/GETTY IMAGES ©

Marin County

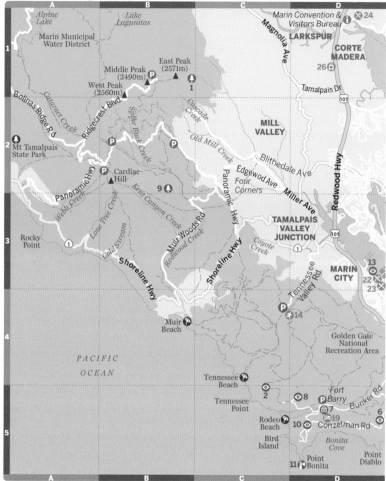

Marine Mammal Center *Animal Rescue Center*
(☎ 415-289-7325; www.marinemammalcenter.org; ⊙10am-5pm; 🚻) FREE Set on the hill above Rodeo Lagoon, the Marine Mammal Center rehabilitates injured, sick and orphaned sea mammals before returning them to the wild, and has educational exhibits about these animals and the dangers they face. During the spring pupping season the center can have up to several dozen orphaned seal pups on site and you can often see them before they're set free.

Headlands Center for the Arts *Gallery*
(☎ 415-331-2787; www.headlands.org; 944 Simmonds Rd; ⊙noon-5pm Sun-Thu) FREE In Fort Barry, refurbished barracks converted into artist work spaces host open studios with its artists-in-residence, as well as talks, performances and other events.

🏃 Activities

Hiking

At the end of Bunker Rd sits Rodeo Beach, protected from wind by high cliffs. From here the Coastal Trail meanders 3.5 miles inland, past abandoned military bunkers, to the Tennessee Valley Trail. It then continues

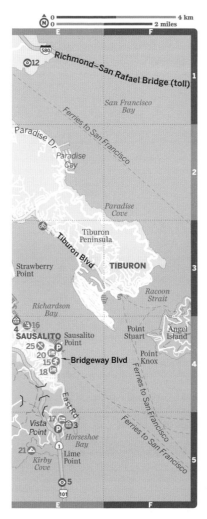

Marin County

◎ Sights

1	Baltimore Canyon	B1
2	Battery Townsley	C5
3	Bay Area Discovery Museum	E5
4	Bay Model Visitor Center	E4
5	Golden Gate Bridge	E5
6	Hawk Hill	D5
7	Headlands Center for the Arts	D5
8	Marine Mammal Center	D5
9	Muir Woods National Monument	B2
10	Nike Missile Site SF-88	D5
	Plaza Viña Del Mar	see 20
11	Point Bonita Lighthouse	D5
12	San Quentin State Penitentiary	E1
13	Sausalito Houseboats	D3

☉ Activities, Courses & Tours

14	Miwok Livery Stables	C4
15	Sausalito Bike Rentals	E4
16	Sea Trek Kayak & SUP	E4

◛ Sleeping

17	Cavallo Point	E5
18	Gables Inn	E4
19	HI Marin Headlands Hostel	D5
20	Hotel Sausalito	E4
	Inn Above Tide	see 20
21	Kirby Cove Campground	E5

✖ Eating

22	Avatar's	D3
23	Fish	D3
24	Marin Brewing Company	D1
	Murray Circle	see 17
25	Sushi Ran	E4

◉ Shopping

26	Book Passage	D1

weekends), especially for families. It has easy, level access to the cove beach and ocean, and is a short 3.8-mile round trip. From Hwy 101, take the Mill Valley–Stinson Beach–Hwy 1 exit and turn left onto Tennessee Valley Rd from the Shoreline Hwy; follow it to the parking lot and trailhead.

Mountain Biking

The Marin Headlands have some excellent mountain-biking routes, and it's an exhilarating ride across the Golden Gate Bridge.

For a good 12-mile dirt loop, choose the Coastal Trail west from the fork of Conzelman and McCullough Rds, winding down to Bunker Rd where it meets Bobcat Trail, which joins Marincello Trail and descends into the Tennessee Valley parking area. The

6 miles along the blustery headlands all the way to Muir Beach.

All along the coastline you'll find cool old battery sites – abandoned concrete bunkers dug into the ground with fabulous views. Evocative Battery Townsley, a half-mile walk or bike ride up from the Fort Cronkite parking lot, opens for free subterranean tours from noon to 4pm on the first Sunday of the month.

Tennessee Valley Trail   Hiking

This trail offers beautiful views of the rugged coastline and is one of the most popular hikes in Marin (expect crowds on

Old Springs Trail and the Miwok Trail take you back to Bunker Rd a bit more gently than the Bobcat Trail, though any attempt to avoid at least a couple of hefty climbs is futile.

Horseback Riding

For a ramble on all fours, Miwok Livery Stables ([☎]415-383-8048; www.miwokstables.com; 701 Tennessee Valley Rd; trail ride $75) offers hillside trail rides with stunning views of Mt Tam and the ocean. Reservations required.

🛏 Sleeping

There are four small campgrounds in the headlands, and two involve hiking (or cycling) in at least 1 mile from the nearest parking lot. Hawk, Bicentennial and Haypress campgrounds are inland, with free camping, but sites must be reserved through the Marin Headlands Visitors Center. None have water available.

Kirby Cove Campground   Campground $

([☎]877-444-6777; www.recreation.gov; tent sites $25; ☺Apr-Oct) In a spectacular shady nook near the entrance to the bay, there's a small beach with the Golden Gate Bridge arching over the rocks nearby. At night you can watch the phantom shadows of cargo ships passing by (and sometimes be lulled to sleep by the dirge of a fog horn). Reserve far ahead.

HI Marin Headlands Hostel   Hostel $

([☎]415-331-2777; www.norcalhostels.org/marin; Fort Barry, Bldg 941; dm $26-30, r $72-92, all with shared bath; [@]) 🖉 Wake up to grazing deer and dew on the ground at this spartan 1907 military compound snuggled in the woods. It has comfortable beds and two well-stocked kitchens, and guests can gather round a fireplace in the common room, shoot pool or play ping-pong. Hiking trails beckon outside.

Cavallo Point   Hotel $$$

([☎]888-651-2003, 415-339-4700; www.cavallopoint.com; 601 Murray Circle; r from $359; [✳][@][🛜][🐾][🐕]) 🖉 Spread out over 45 acres of the Bay Area's most scenic parkland, Cavallo Point is a buzz-worthy lodge that flaunts a green focus, a full-service spa and easy access to outdoor activities. Choose from richly renovated rooms in the landmark Fort Baker officers' quarters or more contemporary solar-powered accommodations with exquisite bay views (including a turret of the Golden Gate Bridge).

❶ Information

Information is available from the **Golden Gate National Recreation Area** (GGNRA; [☎]415-561-4700; www.nps.gov/goga) and the **Marin Headlands Visitors Center** ([☎]415-331-1540; www.nps.gov/goga/marin-headlands.htm; Fort Barry; ☺9:30am-4:30pm), in an old chapel off Bunker Rd near Fort Barry.

❶ Getting There & Away

By car, take the Alexander Ave exit just after the Golden Gate Bridge and dip left under the freeway. Conzelman Rd, to the right, takes you up along the bluffs; you can also take Bunker Rd, which leads to the headlands through a one-way tunnel. It's also a snap to reach these roads from the bridge via bicycle.

Sausalito

Sausalito began as a 19,000-acre land grant to an army captain in 1838. When it became the terminus of the train line down the Pacific Coast, it entered a new stage as a busy lumber port with a racy waterfront. Dramatic changes came in WWII when Sausalito became the site of Marinship, a huge shipbuilding yard. After the war a new bohemian period began, with a resident artists' colony living in 'arks' (houseboats moored along the bay). Hundreds of these floating abodes remain.

Sausalito today is a major tourist haven, jam-packed with souvenir shops and costly boutiques. It's the first town you encounter after crossing the Golden Gate Bridge, so daytime crowds turn up in droves and make parking difficult. Ferrying from San Francisco makes a more relaxing excursion.

⊙ Sights

Sausalito is actually on Richardson Bay, a smaller bay within San Francisco Bay. The commercial district is mainly one street, Bridgeway Blvd, on the waterfront.

Bay Area Discovery Museum Museum
See page 20

★ Sausalito Houseboats Architecture
Bohemia still thrives along the shoreline of Richardson Bay, where free spirits inhabit hundreds of quirky homes that bobble in the waves amongst the seabirds and seals. Structures range from psychedelic mural-splashed castles to dilapidated salt-sprayed shacks and immaculate three-story floating mansions. It's a tight-knit community, where residents tend sprawling dockside gardens and stop to chat on the creaky wooden boardwalks as they wheel their groceries home.

You can poke around the houseboat docks located off Bridgeway between Gate 5 and Gate 6½ Rds.

Bay Model Visitor Center Museum
(☑ 415-332-3871; www.spn.usace.army.mil/Missions/ Recreation/BayModelVisitorCenter.aspx; 2100 Bridgeway Blvd; ⊙ 9am-4pm Tue-Sat, plus 10am-5pm Sat & Sun in summer; ➍) One of the coolest things in town, fascinating to both kids and adults, is the Army Corps of Engineers' solar-powered visitor center. Housed in one of the old (and cold!) Marinship warehouses, it's a 1.5-acre hydraulic model of San Francisco Bay and the delta region. Self-guided tours take you over and around it as the water flows.

Plaza Viña Del Mar Park
Near the ferry terminal, the plaza has a fountain flanked by 14ft-tall elephant statues from the 1915 Panama–Pacific Exposition in San Francisco.

☂ Activities

Sausalito is great for bicycling, whether for a leisurely ride around town, a trip across the Golden Gate Bridge or a longer-haul journey. From the ferry terminal, an easy option is to head south on Bridgeway Blvd, veering left onto East Rd toward the Bay Area Discovery Museum. Another nice route heads north along Bridgeway Blvd, then crosses under Hwy 101 to Mill Valley. At Blithedale Ave, you can veer east to Tiburon; a bike path parallels parts of Tiburon Blvd.

Sea Trek Kayak & SUP Kayaking
(☑ 415-332-8494; www.seatrek.com; Schoonmaker Point Marina; single/double kayaks per hr $20/35) On a nice day, Richardson Bay is irresistible. Kayaks and stand-up paddleboards can be rented here, near the Bay Model Visitor Center. No experience is necessary, and lessons and group outings are also available.

Also on offer are guided kayaking excursions around Angel Island from $75 per person, including overnight camping ($125). Tours include equipment and instructions. May through October is the best time to paddle.

WHY IS IT SO FOGGY?

When the summer sun's rays warm the air over the chilly Pacific, fog forms and hovers offshore; to grasp how it moves inland requires an understanding of California's geography. The vast agricultural region in the state's interior, the Central Valley, is ringed by mountains like a giant bathtub. The only substantial sea-level break in these mountains occurs at the Golden Gate, to the west, which happens to be the direction from which prevailing winds blow. As the inland valley heats up and the warm air rises, it creates a deficit of air at surface level, generating wind that gets sucked through the only opening it can find: the Golden Gate. It happens fast and it's unpredictable. Gusty wind is the only indication that the fog is about to roll in. But even this is inconsistent: there can be fog at the beaches south of the Golden Gate and sun a mile to the north. Hills block fog – especially at times of high atmospheric pressure, as often happens in summer. Because of this, weather forecasters speak of the Bay Area's 'microclimates.' In July it's not uncommon for inland areas to reach 100°F (38°C), while the mercury at the coast barely reaches 70°F (21°C).

DAVID JOYNER/GETTY IMAGES ©

Sausalito Bike Rentals Bicycle Rental

(☑415-331-2453; www.sausalitobikerentals.com; 34a Princess St; bicycle per hour $10; ☺10am-6pm) Rent road, mountain, tandems ($25 per hour) and electric ($20 per hour) bicycles to explore the area.

🛌 Sleeping

All of the lodgings below charge an additional $15 to $20 per night for parking.

Hotel Sausalito Historic Hotel $$

(☑415-332-0700; www.hotelsausalito.com; 16 El Portal; r $180-225, ste $305-320; ✳🖂) Steps away from the ferry in the middle of downtown, this grand 1915 hotel has loads of period charm, paired with modern touches like MP3-player docking stations. Each guest room is decorated in Mediterranean hues, with sumptuous bathrooms and park or partial bay views.

Inn Above Tide Inn $$$

(☑415-332-9535, 800-893-8433; www.innabovetide. com; 30 El Portal; r incl breakfast $345-625, ste $735-1100; ✳@🖂) Next to the ferry terminal, ensconce yourself in one of the 31 modern and spacious rooms – most with private decks and wood-burning fireplaces – that practically levitate over the water. With envy-inducing bay views from your window, scan the horizon with the in-room binoculars. Free loaner bicycles available.

Gables Inn Inn $$$

(☑415-289-1100; www.gablesinnsausalito.com; 62 Princess St; r incl breakfast $199-545; @🖂) Tranquil and inviting, this inn has nine guest rooms in a historic 1869 home, and six in a newer building. The more expensive rooms have spa baths, fireplaces and balconies with spectacular views, but even the smaller, cheaper rooms are stylish and tranquil. Evening wine and cheese is included.

🍴 Eating

Bridgeway Blvd is packed with moderately priced cafes, a few budget ethnic food op-

Golden Gate Bridge

tions and some more expensive bay-view restaurants.

Avatar's
Indian $$

(www.enjoyavatars.com; 2656 Bridgeway Blvd; mains $10-17; ☻11am-3pm & 5-9:30pm Mon-Sat; 🖉🖢) Boasting a cuisine of 'ethnic confusion,' the Indian fusion dishes here incorporate Mexican, Italian and Caribbean ingredients and will bowl you over with their flavor and creativity. Think Punjabi enchilada with curried sweet potato or spinach and mushroom ravioli with mango and rose petal alfredo sauce. All diets (vegan, gluten-free, etc) are graciously accommodated.

Fish
Seafood $$

(☎415-331-3474; www.fish311.com; 350 Harbor Dr; mains $14-28; ☻11:30am-8:30pm; 🖢) 🍃 Chow down on seafood sandwiches, oysters and Dungeness crab roll with organic local butter at redwood picnic tables facing Richardson Bay. A local leader in promoting fresh and sustainably caught fish, this place has wonderful wild salmon in season, and refuses to serve the farmed stuff. Cash only.

Sushi Ran
Japanese $$$

(☎415-332-3620; www.sushiran.com; 107 Caledonia St; sushi $4-33; ☻11:45am-2:30pm Mon-Fri, 5-10pm Sun-Thu, to 11pm Fri & Sat; 🖉) Many Bay Area residents claim this place is the best sushi spot around. If you didn't reserve ahead, the wine and sake bar next door eases the pain of the long wait for a table.

Murray Circle
Modern American $$$

(☎415-339-4750; www.cavallopoint.com/dine.html; 601 Murray Circle, Fort Baker; dinner mains $23-34; ☻7-11am & 11:30am-2pm Mon-Fri, to 2:30pm Sat & Sun, 5:30-10pm Sun-Thu, to 11pm Fri & Sat) At the Cavallo Point lodge, dine on locally sourced meats, seafood and produce, like grass-fed organic beef burgers or Dungeness crab BLT, in a clubby dining room topped by a pressed-tin ceiling. Reservations recommended for dinner.

❶ Information

The **Sausalito Visitors Center** (☎415-332-0505; www.sausalito.org; 780 Bridgeway Blvd; ☻11:30am-4pm Tue-Sun) has local information. There's also an information kiosk at the ferry terminal.

ⓘ Getting There & Away

Driving to Sausalito from San Francisco, take the Alexander Ave exit (the first exit after the Golden Gate Bridge) and follow the signs into Sausalito. There are five municipal parking lots in town, but street parking is difficult to find.

Sir Francis Drake Blvd & Around

The towns along and nearby the Sir Francis Drake Blvd corridor – including Larkspur, Corte Madera, Ross, San Anselmo and Fairfax – evoke charmed small-town life, even though things get busy around Hwy 101.

Starting from the eastern section in Larkspur, window-shop along Magnolia Ave or explore the redwoods in nearby Baltimore Canyon. On the east side of the freeway is the hulking mass of San Quentin State Penitentiary, California's oldest and most notorious prison, founded in 1852. Johnny Cash recorded an album here in 1969 after scoring a big hit with his live *At Folsom Prison* album a few years earlier.

Take the bicycle and pedestrian bridge from the ferry terminal across the road to the Marin Country Mart, a shopping center with a dozen excellent eateries and comfortable outdoor seating. One favorite is the Marin Brewing Company (www.marinbrewing. com; 1809 Larkspur Landing Cir, Marin Country Mart, Bldg 2, Larkspur; mains $12-19; ⊙11:30am-midnight Sun-Thu, to 1am Fri & Sat; 🔊) brewpub, where you can see the glassed-in kettles behind the bar. The head brewer, Arne Johnson, has won many awards, and the Mt Tam Pale Ale complements the menu of pizza, burgers and hearty sandwiches.

Just south, Corte Madera is home to one of the Bay Area's best bookstores, Book Passage (☑ 415-927-0960; www.bookpassage.com; 51 Tamal Vista Blvd; ⊙9am-9pm), in the Marketplace shopping center. It has a strong travel section, plus frequent author appearances.

Continuing west along Sir Francis Drake, San Anselmo has a cute, small downtown area along San Anselmo Ave, including several antique shops. The attractive center of neighboring Fairfax has ample dining and shopping options, and cyclists congregate at Gestalt Haus Fairfax (28 Bolinas Rd, Fairfax; ⊙11:30am-11pm Sun & Mon, 11:30am-midnight Tue & Wed, 11:30am-2am Thu-Sat) for the indoor bicycle parking, board games, European draft beers and sausages of the meaty or vegan persuasion.

Arti (www.articafe.com; 7282 Sir Francis Drake Blvd; mains $10-14; ⊙noon-9pm; ✏) 🖊, between Hwys 1 and 101 in the tiny hamlet of Lagunitas, is a tempting stop for organic Indian fare. There's a cozy, casual dining room and an outdoor patio for warm days, and folks from miles around adore its sizzling chicken tikka platter.

Six miles east of Olema on Sir Francis Drake Blvd, Samuel P Taylor State Park (☑ 415-488-9897; www.parks.ca.gov/?page_id=469; parking $8, tent & RV sites $35, cabin $100) has beautiful, secluded campsites in redwood groves and a coveted handful of new five-person cabins with electricity and wood stoves. The park's also located on the paved Cross Marin Trail, with miles of creekside landscape to explore along a former railroad grade.

Muir Woods National Monument

Muir Woods   Forest

(See page 20) The 1-mile Main Trail Loop is a gentle walk alongside Redwood Creek to the 1000-year-old trees at Cathedral Grove; it returns via Bohemian Grove, where the tallest tree in the park stands 254ft high. The Dipsea Trail is a good 2-mile hike up to the top of aptly named Cardiac Hill.

You can also walk down into Muir Woods by taking trails from the Panoramic Hwy, such as the Bootjack Trail from the Bootjack picnic area, or from Mt Tamalpais' Pantoll Station campground, along the Ben Johnson Trail.

ⓘ Getting There & Away

The parking lot is insanely full during busy periods, so consider taking the seasonal **Muir Woods Shuttle** (Route 66F; www.marintransit. org; round trip adult/child $5/free; ⊙weekends & holidays late-Mar–Oct). The 40-minute shuttle connects with Sausalito ferries arriving from San Francisco before 3pm.

To get there by car, drive north on Hwy 101, exit at Hwy 1 and continue north along Hwy 1/ Shoreline Hwy to the Panoramic Hwy (a right-hand fork). Follow that for about 1 mile to Four Corners, where you turn left onto Muir Woods Rd (there are plenty of signs).

Bolinas

For a town that is so famously unexcited about tourism, Bolinas offers some fairly tempting attractions for the visitor. The highway department used to put signs up at the turnoff from Hwy 1; locals kept taking them down, so the highway department finally gave up.

⊙ Sights & Activities

★ Point Blue
Conservation Science   Bird Observatory
(✑ 415-868-0655; www.pointblue.org) Off Mesa Rd west of downtown and formerly known as the Point Reyes Bird Observatory, its Palomarin Field Station has bird-banding and netting demonstrations, a visitors center and nature trail. Banding demonstrations are held in the morning every Tuesday to Sunday from May to late November, and on Wednesday, Saturday and Sunday the rest of the year.

Bolinas Museum   Museum
(✑ 415-868-0330; www.bolinasmuseum.org; 48 Wharf Rd; ⊙1-5pm Fri, noon-5pm Sat & Sun) **FREE** This courtyard complex of five galleries exhibits local artists and showcases the region's history. Look for the weathered Bolinas highway sign affixed to the wall, since you certainly didn't see one on your way into town.

Agate Beach   Beach
There are tide pools along some 2 miles of coastline at Agate Beach, around the end of Duxbury Point.

Bass Lake & Alamere Falls   Hiking
See page 21–2

2 Mile Surf Shop   Surfing
(✑ 415-868-0264; www.2milesurf.com; 22 Brighton Ave; ⊙9am-6pm May-Oct, 10am-5pm Nov-Apr) Surfing's popular in these parts, and this shop behind the post office rents boards and wetsuits and also gives lessons. Call ✑ 415-868-2412 for the surf report.

⌂ Sleeping & Eating

Smiley's Schooner Saloon & Hotel   Motel **$$**
(✑ 415-868-1311; www.smileyssaloon.com; 41 Wharf Rd; r $104-124; 🖥🐾) A crusty old place dating back to 1851, Smiley's has simple but decent rooms, and last-minute weekday rates can be a bargain. The bar, which serves some food, has live bands Thursday through Sat-

urday and is frequented by plenty of salty dogs and grizzled deadheads.

Bolinas People's Store   Cafe, Market **$**
(14 Wharf Rd; ⊙8:30am-6:30pm; 🖥) 🐾 An awesome little co-op grocery store hidden behind the community center, the People's Store serves Fair Trade coffee and sells organic produce, fresh soup and excellent tamales. Eat at the tables in the shady courtyard, and have a rummage through the Free Box, a shed full of clothes and other waiting-to-be-reused items.

Coast Café   American **$$**
(www.bolinascoastcafe.com; 46 Wharf Rd; mains $10-22; ⊙11:30am-3pm & 5-8pm Tue-Thu, to 9pm Fri, 8am-3pm & 5-9pm Sat, to 8pm Sun; 🖥🖮) 🐾 At the only 'real' restaurant in town, everyone jockeys for outdoor seats among the flowerboxes for fish and chips, barbecued oysters, or buttermilk pancakes with damn good coffee. Live music Thursday and Sunday nights.

❶ Getting There & Away
Route 61 of the **West Marin Stagecoach** (✑ 415-526-3239; www.marintransit.org/stage.html) goes daily ($2) from the Marin City transit hub (weekend and holiday service from the Sausalito ferry) to downtown Bolinas. By car, follow Hwy 1 north from Stinson Beach and turn west for Bolinas at the first road north of the lagoon. At the first stop sign, take another left onto Olema–Bolinas Rd and follow it 2 miles to town.

Point Reyes Station
Though the railroad stopped coming through in 1933 and the town is small, Point Reyes Station is nevertheless the hub of west Marin. Dominated by dairies and ranches, the region was invaded by artists in the 1960s. Today it's an interesting blend of art galleries and tourist shops. The town has a rowdy saloon and the occasional smell of cattle on the afternoon breeze.

⌂ Sleeping & Eating
Cute little cottages, cabins and B&Bs are plentiful in and around Point Reyes. The West Marin Chamber of Commerce (✑ 415-663-9232; www.pointreyes.org) has numerous listings, as does the Point Reyes Lodging Association (✑ 415-663-1872, 800-539-1872; www.ptreyes.com).

Muir Woods National Monument
DANITA DELIMONT/GETY IMAGES ©

Windsong Cottage Guest Yurt   Yurt $$

(☑ 415-663-9695; www.windsongcottage.com; 25 McDonald Lane; d yurt $185-210; ☎) A wood-burning stove, private outdoor hot tub, comfy king bed and kitchen stocked with breakfast supplies make this round sky-lighted abode a cozy slice of heaven.

Bovine Bakery   Bakery $

(www.thebovinebakery.com; 11315 Hwy 1; pastry $3; ⊙ 6:30am-5pm Mon-Fri, 7am-5pm Sat & Sun) ✐ Don't leave town without sampling something buttery from possibly the best bakery in Marin. A sweet bear-claw pastry and an organic coffee are a good way to kick off your morning.

Tomales Bay Foods &
Cowgirl Creamery   Deli, Market $

(www.cowgirlcreamery.com; 80 4th St; sandwiches $6-12; ⊙ 10am-6pm Wed-Sun; ☑) ✐ A market in an old barn selling picnic items, including gourmet cheeses and organic produce. Reserve a spot in advance for the small-scale artisanal cheesemaker's demonstration and tasting ($5); watch the curd-making and cutting, then sample a half dozen of the fresh and aged cheeses. All of the milk is local and organic, with vegetarian rennet in the soft cheeses.

Osteria Stellina   Italian $$

(☑ 415-663-9988; www.osteriastellina.com; 11285 Hwy 1; mains $15-24; ⊙ 11:30am-2:30pm & 5-9pm; ☑) ✐ This place specializes in rustic Italian cuisine made from locally sourced produce, including pizza and pasta dishes and Niman Ranch meats. For dessert, the water-buffalo-milk gelato is the way to go.

Pine Cone Diner   Diner $$

(www.pineconediner.com; 60 4th St; mains $9-13; ⊙ 8am-2:30pm; ☑) ✐ The Pine Cone serves big breakfasts and lunches inside a cute retro dining room and at shaded al fresco picnic tables. Try the buttermilk biscuits, the chorizo or tofu scramble, or the fried oyster sandwich.

☆ Entertainment

Old Western Saloon   Live Music, Bar

(☑ 415-663-1661; cnr Shoreline Hwy & 2nd St; ⊙ 10am-midnight or 2am) A rustic 1906 saloon with live bands and cool tables emblazoned with horseshoes. Prince Charles stopped in here for an impromptu pint during a local visit in 2006.

❶ Getting There & Away

Hwy 1 becomes Main St in town, running right through the center.

Point Reyes National Seashore

The windswept peninsula Point Reyes (www.nps.gov/pore) FREE is a rough-hewn beauty that has always lured marine mammals and migratory birds as well as scores of shipwrecks. It was here in 1579 that Sir Francis Drake landed to repair his ship, the *Golden Hind*. During his five-week stay he mounted a brass plaque near the shore claiming this land for England. Historians believe this occurred at Drakes Beach and there is a marker there today. In 1595 the first of scores of ships lost in these waters, the *San Augustine,* went down. She was a Spanish treasure ship out of Manila laden with luxury goods, and to this day bits of her cargo wash up on shore. Despite modern navigation, the dangerous waters here continue to claim the odd boat.

Point Reyes National Seashore has 110 square miles of pristine ocean beaches, and the peninsula offers excellent hiking and camping opportunities. Be sure to bring warm clothing, as even the sunniest days can quickly turn cold and foggy.

◉ Sights & Activities

For an awe-inspiring view, follow the Earthquake Trail from the park headquarters at Bear Valley. The trail reaches a 16ft gap between the two halves of a once-connected fence line, a lasting testimonial to the power of the 1906 earthquake that was centered in this area. Another trail leads from the visitors center a short way to Kule Loklo, a reproduction of a Miwok village.

Limantour Rd, off Bear Valley Rd about 1 mile north of Bear Valley Visitor Center, leads to the Point Reyes Hostel and Limantour Beach, where a trail runs along Limantour Spit with Estero de Limantour on one side and Drakes Bay on the other. The Inverness Ridge Trail heads from Limantour Rd up to Mt Vision (1282ft), from where there are spectacular views of the entire national seashore. You can drive almost to the top of Mt Vision from the other side.

About 2 miles past Inverness, Pierce Point Rd splits off to the right from Sir Francis Drake Blvd. From here you can get to two nice swimming beaches on the bay: Marshall Beach requires a mile-long hike from the parking area, while Hearts Desire, in Tomales Bay State Park, is accessible by car.

Pierce Point Rd continues to the huge windswept sand dunes at Abbotts Lagoon, full of peeping killdeer and other shorebirds. At the end of the road is Pierce Point Ranch, the trailhead for the 3.5-mile Tomales Point Trail through the Tule Elk Reserve. The plentiful elk are an amazing sight, standing with their big horns against the backdrop of Tomales Point, with Bodega Bay to the north, Tomales Bay to the east and the Pacific Ocean to the west.

★ Point Reyes Lighthouse   Lighthouse

(⊙ lighthouse 10am-4:30pm Fri-Mon, lens room 2:30-4pm Fri-Mon) FREE The lighthouse sits below the headlands; to reach it requires descending more than 300 stairs. Nearby Chimney Rock is a fine short hike, especially in spring when the wildflowers are blossoming. A nearby viewing area allows you to spy on the park's elephant seal colony.

Keep back from the water's edge at the exposed North Beach and South Beach, as people have been dragged in and drowned by frequent rogue waves.

Five Brooks Stables   Horseback Riding

(☑ 415-663-1570; www.fivebrooks.com; trail rides from $40; 🐴) Explore the landscape on horseback with a trail ride. Take a slow amble through a pasture or ascend more than 1000ft to Inverness Ridge for views of the Olema Valley. If you can stay in the saddle

for six hours, ride along the coastline to Alamere Falls via Wildcat Beach.

🛏 Sleeping

Wake up to deer nibbling under a blanket of fog at one of Point Reyes' four very popular hike-in campgrounds (☑ 877-444-6777; www.recreation.gov; tent sites $20), each with pit toilets, water and tables. Reservations are accepted up to six months in advance, and weekends go fast. Reaching the campgrounds requires a 2- to 6-mile hike or bicycle ride, or you can try for a permit to camp on the beach in Tomales Bay. Check with the Bear Valley Visitor Center for same-day permits.

★ HI Point Reyes Hostel   Hostel $

(☑ 415-663-8811; www.norcalhostels.org/reyes; 1390 Limantour Spit Rd; dm $25, r $82-120, all with shared bath; @) ♠ Just off Limantour Rd, this rustic Hostelling International property has bunkhouses with warm and cozy front rooms, big-view windows and outdoor areas with hill vistas. A newer LEED-certified building has four private rooms (two-night minimum stay on weekends) and a stunning modern kitchen. It's in a secluded valley 2 miles from the ocean and surrounded by lovely hiking trails.

ⓘ Information

The park headquarters, **Bear Valley Visitor Center** (☑ 415-464-5100; www.nps.gov/pore; ⊙ 10am-5pm Mon-Fri, from 9am Sat & Sun), is near Olema and has information and maps. You can also get information at the Point Reyes Lighthouse and the **Kenneth Patrick Center** (☑ 415-669-1250; ⊙ 9:30am-4:30pm Sat, Sun & holidays) at Drakes Beach. All visitor centers have slightly longer hours in summer.

ⓘ Getting There & Away

By car you can get to Point Reyes a few different ways. The curviest is along Hwy 1, through Stinson Beach and Olema. More direct is to exit Hwy 101 in San Rafael and follow Sir Francis Drake Blvd all the way to the tip of Point Reyes. For the latter route, take the central San Rafael exit and head west on 4th St, which turns into Sir Francis Drake Blvd. By either route, it's about 1½ hours to Olema from San Francisco.

Just north of Olema, where Hwy 1 and Sir Francis Drake Blvd come together, is Bear Valley Rd; turn left to reach the Bear Valley Visitor Center. If you're heading to the further reaches of Point Reyes, follow Sir Francis Drake Blvd through Point Reyes Station and out onto the peninsula (about an hour's drive).

Napa & Sonoma Wine Country

Despite hype about Wine Country style, it's from the land that all Wine Country lore springs.

Rolling hills, dotted with century-old oaks, turn the color of lion's fur under the summer sun and swaths of vineyards carpet hillsides as far as the eye can see. Where they end, lush redwood forests follow serpentine rivers to the sea.

There are over 600 wineries in Napa and Sonoma Counties, but it's quality, not quantity, that sets the region apart – especially in Napa, which competes with France and doubles as an outpost of San Francisco's top-end culinary scene. Sonoma prides itself on agricultural diversity, with goat-cheese farms, you-pick-'em orchards and roadside fruit stands. Plan to get lost on back roads, and, as you picnic atop sun-dappled hillsides, grab a hunk of earth and know firsthand the thing of greatest meaning in Wine Country.

NAPA VALLEY

The birthplace of modern-day Wine Country is famous for regal Cabernet Sauvignons, château-like wineries and fabulous food, attracting more than four million visitors a year, many planning to wine and dine themselves into a stupor, maybe get a massage, and sleep somewhere swell with fine linens and a pool.

The city of Napa anchors the valley, but the real work happens up-valley. Napa isn't as pretty as other towns, but has some noteworthy sights, among them Oxbow Public

Market. Scenic towns include St Helena, Yountville and Calistoga – the latter more famous for water than wine.

Napa Valley Wineries

★ **Hess Collection** Winery, Gallery
(707-255-1144; www.hesscollection.com; 4411 Redwood Rd, Napa; tasting $15, gallery free; 10am-5:30pm) Art lovers: don't miss Hess Collection, whose galleries display mixed-media and large-canvas works, including pieces by Francis Bacon and Louis Soutter. In the cave-like tasting room, find well-known Cabernet and Chardonnay, but also try the Viognier. Hess overlooks the valley: be prepared to drive a winding road. Reservations recommended. Bottles: $20 to $60. (NB: Don't confuse Hess Collection with Hess Select, the grocery-store brand.)

Darioush Winery
See page 33

Regusci Winery
See page 33

Robert Sinskey Winery
See page 23

Robert Mondavi Winery
See page 23

Mumm Napa   Winery, Gallery
See page 28

★ **Frog's Leap**   Winery
See page 28

★ **Tres Sabores**   Winery
(☑707-967-8027; www.tressabores.com; 1620 South
Whitehall Lane, St Helena; tour & tasting $20; ☺by
appointment; 🖭) ✍ At the valley's western-
most edge, where sloping vineyards meet
wooded hillsides, Tres Sabores is a portal to
old Napa – no fancy tasting room, no snobbery, just great wine in a spectacular setting.
Bucking the Cabernet custom, Tres Sabores
crafts elegantly structured, Burgundian-style
Zinfandel, and spritely Sauvignon Blanc,
which the *New York Times* dubbed a top 10
of its kind in California. Reservations essential.

Guinea fowl and sheep control pests on
the 35-acre estate, while golden labs chase
butterflies through gnarled old vines. After
your tour, linger at olive-shaded picnic tables
and drink in gorgeous valley views. Bottles
cost $22 to $80.

Hall   Winery
See page 28

Castello di Amorosa   Winery, Castle
See page 31

Lava Vine   Winery
See page 33

Napa
See page 27

◉ Sights
**di Rosa Art +
Nature Preserve**   Gallery, Gardens
See page 27

☞ Tours
Napa Valley Wine Train   Train Tour
(☑800-427-4124, 707-253-2111; www.winetrain.
com; adult/child from $109/74) A cushy, if tour-
isty, way to see Wine Country, the Wine
Train offers three-hour daily trips in vintage
Pullman dining cars, from Napa to St Helena and back, with an optional winery tour.
Trains depart from McKinstry St, near 1st St.

🛏 Sleeping
Summer demand exceeds supply. Weekend
rates skyrocket. Also consider staying in
Calistoga (p91).

Chablis Inn   Motel $$
(☑707-257-1944; www.chablisinn.com; 3360
Solano Ave; r Mon-Fri $89-109, Sat & Sun $169-189;
❄@🛰🏊) Good-value, well-kept motel near
Napa's only stretch of freeway. Hot tub.

IMAGE SOURCE/GETTY IMAGES ©

Napa Valley vineyards

TOP TIP: CUTTING COSTS IN NAPA

To avoid overspending on tasting fees, it's perfectly acceptable to pay for one tasting to share between two people. Ask in advance if fees are applicable to purchase (they usually aren't).

Tour fees cannot be split. Ask at your hotel, or at visitors centers, for free- or discounted-tasting coupons, or download from napatouristguide.com. If you can't afford the hotels, try western Sonoma County, but if you want to be nearer Napa, try the suburban towns of Vallejo and American Canyon, about 20 minutes from downtown Napa. Both have motels for $75 to $125 in high season. Also find chains 30 minutes away in Fairfield, off I-80 exits 41 (Pittman Rd) and 45 (Travis Blvd).

★ Carneros Inn
Resort $$$

(☏707-299-4900; www.thecarnerosinn.com; 4048 Sonoma Hwy; r Mon-Fri $485-570, Sat & Sun $650-900; ❋@🖰❄🐾) Carneros Inn's contemporary aesthetic and retro, small-town agricultural theme shatter the predictable Wine Country mold. The semi-detached, corrugated-metal cottages look like itinerant housing, but inside they're snappy and chic, with cherry-wood floors, ultrasuede headboards, wood-burning fireplaces, heated-tile bathroom floors, giant tubs and indoor-outdoor showers. Linger by day at the hilltop pool, by night at the outdoor fireplaces. Two excellent on-site restaurants.

Milliken Creek Inn
Inn $$$

(☏888-622-5775, 707-255-1197; www.millikencreekinn.com; 1815 Silverado Trail; r incl breakfast $295-750; ❋@🖰) Understatedly elegant Milliken Creek combines small-inn charm, fine-hotel service and B&B intimacy. Rooms are impeccably styled in English-Colonial style, and have top-flight amenities, fireplaces and ultra-high-thread-count linens. Breakfast is delivered. Book a river-view room.

✕ Eating

Make reservations whenever possible. July to mid-August, look for the peach stand at Deer Park Rd and Silverado Trail (across Deer Park Rd from Stewart's farmstand) for juicy, delicious heirloom varieties.

★ Oxbow Public Market
Market $

(See also p27) Standouts: Hog Island oysters (six for $16); comfort cooking at celeb-chef Todd Humphries' Kitchen Door (mains $14 to $24); Venezuelan cornbread sandwiches ($9) at Pica Pica; great Cal-Mexican at C Casa (tacos $5 to $9); pastries at Ca'Momi ($2); and Three Twins certified-organic ice cream ($3.75 for a single cone).

Alexis Baking Co
Cafe $

(☏707-258-1827; www.alexisbakingcompany.com; 1517 3rd St; dishes $7-13; ☉7am-3pm Mon-Fri, 7:30am-3pm Sat, 8am-2pm Sun; 🖉🖰) Our fave spot for quality scrambles, granola, focaccia, big cups of joe and boxed lunches to go.

Taqueria Maria
Mexican $

(☏707-257-6925; www.taqueriamaria.com; 640 3rd St; mains $8-13; ☉9am-8:30pm Sun-Thu, to 9pm Fri & Sat; 🖉🖰) Reliably good Mexican cooking that won't break the bank. Also serves breakfast.

Oenotri
Italian $$

(☏707-252-1022; www.oenotri.com; 1425 1st St; dinner mains $17-29, lunch $13-15; ☉11:30am-2:30pm & 5:30-9pm Sun-Thu, to 10pm Fri & Sat) 🖉 Housemade salumi and pastas, and wood-fired Naples-style pizzas are the stars at always-busy Oenotri, which draws crowds for daily-changing, locally sourced, rustic-Italian cooking, served in a cavernous brick-walled space.

Carpe Diem Wine Bar
Californian $$

(☏707-224-0800; www.carpediemwinebar.com; 1001 2nd St; mains $17-19; ☉4-9pm Mon-Thu, to 10pm Fri & Sat) This busy storefront wine bar and restaurant makes inventive, flavorful small plates, from simple skewers and flatbreads, to elaborate ostrich burgers, salumi platters and – wait for it – duck confit 'quack and cheese.'

Torc
Californian $$$

(☏707-252-3292; www.torcnapa.com; 1140 Main St; mains $26-29; ☉5-9:30pm daily, 10:30am-2:30pm Sat & Sun) Wildly popular Torc plays off the seasons with dynamic combinations of farm-fresh ingredients, such as springtime white asparagus with black-truffle toasts, and squab with artichoke and licorice. Well-arranged for people-watching, the big stone dining room has an open-truss ceiling, and exposed pine-wood tables that downplay formality. Reservations essential.

Bistro Don Giovanni   Italian $$$

(☑707-224-3300; www.bistrodongiovanni.com; 4110 Howard Lane; mains $16-28; ☉11:30am-10pm Sun-Thu, to 11pm Fri & Sat) This long-running favorite roadhouse serves modern-Italian pastas, crispy pizzas and wood-roasted meats. Reservations essential. Weekends get packed – and loud. Request a vineyard-view table (good luck).

🍷 Drinking & Nightlife

Empire   Lounge

(☑707-254-8888; www.empirenapa.com; 1400 1st St; ☉5:30pm-midnight Tue-Thu, to 2am Fri & Sat) Moody and dark, with candlelight and a jellyfish tank, Empire mimics big-city lounges, with good cocktails and uptempo music. Alas, no dance floor.

Billco's Billiards & Darts   Sports Bar

(www.billcos.com; 1234 3rd St; ☉noon-midnight) Dudes in khakis swill craft beers and throw darts inside this polite pool hall.

Downtown Joe's   Sports Bar, Brewery

(www.downtownjoes.com; 902 Main St at 2nd St; 🎤) Live music Thursday to Sunday, TV-sports nightly. Often packed, usually messy.

☆ Entertainment

Silo's Jazz Club   Live Music

(☑707-251-5833; www.silosjazzclub.com; 530 Main St; cover varies; ☉6-10pm Wed-Thu, 7pm-midnight Fri & Sat, varied hrs Sun) A cabaret-style wine-and-beer bar, Silo's hosts jazz and rock acts Friday and Saturday nights; Wednesday and Thursday it's good for drinks. Reservations recommended weekends.

**City Winery at Napa
Valley Opera House**   Theater

(☑707-260-1600; www.citywinery.com/napa; 1030 Main St) Napa's vintage-1880s opera theater houses a happening wine bar and restaurant downstairs, and 300-seat cabaret upstairs, hosting acts like Ginger Baker and Graham Nash. Opening hours vary, though it's usually open Thursday to Sunday evenings.

Uptown Theatre   Theater

(☑707-259-0333; www.uptowntheatrenapa.com; 1350 3rd St) Big-name acts play this restored 1937 theater.

🛍 Shopping

Betty's Girl   Women's Clothing, Vintage

(☑707-254-7560; www.bettysgirlnapa.com; 968 Pearl St; ☉11am-6pm Thu & Fri, 10am-2pm Sat) Expert couturier Kim Northrup fits women with fabulous vintage cocktail dresses and

NAPA OR SONOMA?

Napa and Sonoma Valleys run parallel, separated by the narrow, imposing Mayacamas Mountains. The two couldn't be more different. It's easy to mock aggressively sophisticated Napa, with its monuments to ego, trophy homes and trophy wives, $1000-a-night inns, $50-plus tastings and wine-snob visitors, but Napa makes some of the world's best wines. Constrained by its geography, it stretches along a single valley, making it easy to visit. Drawbacks are high prices and heavy traffic, but there are 400 nearly side-by-side wineries. And the valley is gorgeous.

There are three Sonomas: the town of Sonoma, which is in Sonoma Valley, which is in Sonoma County. Think of them as Russian dolls. Sonoma County is much more down-to-earth and politically left-leaning. Though it's becoming gentrified, Sonoma lacks Napa's chic factor (Healdsburg notwithstanding), and locals like it that way. The wines are more approachable, but the county's 260 wineries are spread out. If you're here on a weekend, head to Sonoma (County or Valley), which gets less traffic, but on a weekday, see Napa, too. Ideally schedule two to four days: one for each valley, and one or two additional for western Sonoma County.

Spring and fall are the best times to visit. Summers are hot, dusty and crowded. Fall brings fine weather, harvest time and the 'crush,' the pressing of the grapes, but lodging prices skyrocket.

0 ——— 2 km
0 ——— 1 miles

Napa Valley North

◉ Sights
1	Castello di Amorosa	A3
2	Hall	A7
3	Lava Vine	B1
4	Old Faithful Geyser	A1
5	Silverado Museum	B7

🏃 Activities, Courses & Tours
6	Calistoga Spa Hot Springs	A2
7	Culinary Institute of America at Greystone	A6
8	Dr Wilkinson's Hot Springs Resort	A2
9	Indian Springs Spa	A2
10	Mount View Spa	A2
11	Spa Solage	B2

custom-made designs, altering and shipping for no additional charge. Open extra hours by appointment.

Napa Valley Olive Oil Mfg Co Food
(nvoliveoil.com; 1331 1st St; ⊘10am-5:30pm) Sample 30 varieties of fine olive oil and vinegar at this downtown specialty-food boutique, which also carries fancy salts and local jam.

❶ Information

Napa Library (☏707-253-4241; www.countyofnapa.org/Library; 580 Coombs St; ⊘10am-9pm Mon-Thu, to 6pm Fri & Sat; 🛜) Free internet access.

Napa Valley Welcome Center (☏707-251-5895, lodging assistance 707-251-9188, toll free 855-847-6272; www.visitnapavalley.com; 600 Main St; ⊘9am-5pm; 🚹) Lodging assistance, wine-tasting passes, spa deals and comprehensive winery maps.

Queen of the Valley Medical Center (☏707-252-4411; www.thequeen.org; 1000 Trancas St; ⊘24hr) Emergency medical.

❶ Getting Around

Pedi cabs park outside downtown restaurants – especially at the foot of Main St, near the Napa Valley Welcome Center – in summertime. The car-sharing service **Uber** (www.uber.com) also operates in Napa.

Yountville

(See page 27) Napa, St Helena and Calistoga are more interesting bases. Most businesses are on Washington St.

NAPA & SONOMA WINE COUNTRY YOUNTVILLE

👁 Sights

Ma(i)sonry Gallery, Tasting Room
See page 27

Napa Valley Museum Museum
See page 27

🛏 Sleeping

Napa Valley Railway Inn Inn $$
(☎ 707-944-2000; www.napavalleyrailwayinn.com; 6523 Washington St; r $125-260; ❊ @ 🛜 🏊) Sleep in a converted railroad car, part of two short trains parked at a central platform. They've little privacy, but come moderately priced. Bring earplugs.

Maison Fleurie B&B $$$
(☎ 800-788-0369, 707-944-2056; www.maisonfleurie napa.com; 6529 Yount St; r incl breakfast $160-295; ❊ @ 🛜 🏊) Rooms at this ivy-covered country inn are in a century-old home and carriage house, decorated in French-provincial style. Big breakfasts, afternoon wine and *hors d'oeuvres,* hot tub.

Bardessono Luxury Hotel $$$
(☎ 877-932-5333, 707-204-6000; www.bardessono. com; 6524 Yount St; r $600-800, ste from $800; ❊ @ 🛜 🏊) 🏊 The outdoors flows indoors at California's first-ever (for what it's worth) LEED-platinum-certified green hotel, made of recycled everything, styled in Japanese-led austerity, with neutral tones and hard angles that are exceptionally urban for farm country. Glam pool deck and on-site spa. Tops for a splurge.

Poetry Inn Inn $$$
(☎ 707-944-0646; www.poetryinn.com; 6380 Silverado Trail; r incl breakfast $650-1400; ❊ 🛜 🏊) There's no better valley view than from this contemporary three-room inn, high on the hills east of Yountville. Decorated with posh restraint, rooms have private balconies, wood-burning fireplaces, 1000-thread-count linens and enormous baths with indoor-outdoor showers. Bring a ring.

🍴 Eating

Make reservations or you may not eat. Yountville Park (cnr Washington & Madison Sts) has picnic tables and barbecue grills. Find groceries across from the post office. There's a great taco truck (6764 Washington St) parked in town.

Bouchon Bakery Bakery $
(☎ 707-944-2253; http://bouchonbakery.com; 6528 Washington St; items from $3; ⊙ 7am-7pm) Bouchon makes as-good-as-in-Paris French pastries and strong coffee. There's always a line and rarely a seat: get it to go.

Napa Style Paninoteca Cafe $
(☎ 707-945-1229; www.napastyle.com; 6525 Washington St; dishes $8-10; ⊙ 11am-3pm) TV-chef Michael Chiarello's cafe (inside his store, Napa Style) makes camera-ready salads and paninos – try the slow-roasted pork – that pair nicely with his organic wines.

Redd Wood Italian $$
(☎ 707-299-5030; www.redd-wood.com; 6755 Washington St; pizzas $12-16, mains $24-28; ⊙ 11:30am-3pm & 5-10pm, to 11pm Fri & Sat) Celeb-chef Richard Reddington's casual Italian trattoria serves outstanding homemade pastas, salumi, and tender-to-the-tooth pizzas from a wood-fired oven.

⭐ French Laundry Californian $$$
(☎ 707-944-2380; www.frenchlaundry.com; 6640 Washington St; prix-fixe dinner $295; ⊙ seatings 11am-1pm Fri-Sun, 5:30pm-9:15pm daily) The pinnacle of California dining, Thomas Keller's French Laundry is epic, a high-wattage culinary experience on par with the world's best. Book two months ahead at 10am sharp, or log onto OpenTable.com precisely at midnight. Avoid tables before 7pm; first-service seating moves a touch quickly.

Bouchon French $$$
(☎ 707-944-8037; www.bouchonbistro.com; 6354 Washington St; mains $19-45; ⊙ 11am-midnight Mon-Fri, from 10am Sat & Sun) Details at celeb-chef Thomas Keller's French brasserie are so impeccable you'd swear you were in Paris. Only the Bermuda-shorts-clad Americans look out of place. On the menu: oysters, onion soup, roasted chicken, leg of lamb, trout with almonds, runny cheeses and perfect profiteroles.

🍷 Drinking & Entertainment

Pancha's Dive Bar
(6764 Washington St; ⊙ noon-2am) Swill tequila with vineyard-workers early, waiters later.

Lincoln Theater Theater
(☎ box office 707-949-9900; www.lincolntheater. org; 100 California Dr) Various artists, including Napa Valley Symphony, play this theater.

Napa Valley Museum (p27)

🛍 Shopping

Napa Style   Food
(📞 707-945-1229; www.napastyle.com; 6525 Washington St; ⏲ 10am-6pm) The only worthwhile store at Yountville's V Martketplace is this fancy cookware shop by celeb-chef Michael Chiarello.

Oakville & Rutherford

See page 27

🛏 Sleeping & Eating

You won't find any budget lodging in Yountville.

⭐ Auberge du Soleil   Luxury Hotel $$$
(📞 800-348-5406, 707-963-1211; www.aubergedusoleil.com; 180 Rutherford Hill Rd, Rutherford; r $850-1200, ste $1500-4000; ❄ 🛜 🏊) The top splurge for a no-holds-barred romantic weekend. A meal in its dining room (breakfast mains $16 to $19, lunch $31 to $42, three-/four-/six-course prix-fixe dinner $105/125/150) is an iconic Napa experience: come for a fancy breakfast, lazy lunch or will-you-wear-my-ring dinner. Valley views are mesmerizing – *don't* sit inside. Make reservations; arrive before sunset.

Rancho Caymus   Hotel $$$
(📞 800-845-1777, 707-963-1777; www.ranchocaymus.com; 1140 Rutherford Rd, Rutherford; r $179-299; ❄ @ 🛜 🏊) Styled after California's missions, this hacienda-like inn scores high marks for its fountain courtyard, kiva fireplaces, oak-beamed ceilings, and comparitively great rates.

La Luna Market & Taqueria   Market $
(📞 707-963-3211; 1153 Rutherford Rd, Rutherford; dishes $4-6; ⏲ 9am-5pm May-Nov) Vineyard workers flock here for burrito lunches and homemade hot sauce.

Oakville Grocery   Deli, Market $$
(📞 707-944-8802; www.oakvillegrocery.com; 7856 Hwy 29, Oakville; sandwiches $9-15; ⏲ 6:30am-5pm) The definitive Wine Country deli: excellent cheeses, charcuterie, bread, olives and wine – however pricy. Find tables outside or ask where to picnic nearby.

Rutherford Grill   American $$
(📞 707-963-1792; www.rutherfordgrill.com; 1180 Rutherford Rd, Rutherford; mains $15-30) Yes, it's a chain, but its bar provides a chance to rub shoulders with winemakers at lunchtime. The food is consistent – ribs, rotisserie chicken, grilled artichokes – and there's no corkage, so bring that bottle you just bought.

St Helena

See page 28

👁 Sights & Activities

Silverado Museum   Museum
See page 29

**Culinary Institute of America
at Greystone**   Cooking Course
See page 29

🛏 Sleeping

El Bonita   Motel $$
(📞707-963-3216; www.elbonita.com; 195 Main St;
r $169-239; ✴@🛜♨🐾) Book in advance to
secure this sought-after motel, with up-to-
date rooms (quietest are in back), attractive
grounds, hot tub and sauna.

Wydown Hotel   Boutique Hotel $$$
(📞707-963-5100; www.wydownhotel.com; 1424 Main
St; r Mon-Fri $269-380, Sat & Sun $379-475; ✴🛜)
Opened in 2012, this fashion-forward boutique hotel, with good service, sits smack
downtown, its 12 oversized rooms smartly
decorated with tufted velvet, distressed
leather, subway-tile baths, and California-
king beds with white-on-white high-thread-
count linens.

Harvest Inn   Inn $$$
(📞707-963-9463, 800-950-8466; www.harvestinn.
com; 1 Main St; r incl breakfast $369-569;
✴@🛜♨🐾) 🌿 A former estate, this 74-room
resort has rooms in satellite buildings on
sprawling manicured grounds. The newest
building's generic; choose the vineyard-view
rooms, which have private hot tubs.

🍴 Eating

Make reservations where possible.

Napa Valley Olive Oil Mfg Co   Market $
(📞707-963-4173; www.oliveoilsainthelena.com; 835
Charter Oak Ave; ⏲8am-5:30pm) Before the ad-
vent of fancy-food stores, this ramshackle
market introduced Napa to Italian delica-
cies – real prosciutto and salami, meaty
olives, fresh bread, nutty cheeses and, of
course, olive oil. Ask nicely and the owner
will lend you a knife and a board to picnic
at the rickety tables in the grass outside.
Cash only.

Sunshine Foods   Market, Deli $
(www.sunshinefoodsmarket.com; 1115 Main St;
⏲7:30am-8:30pm) Town's best grocery store;
excellent deli.

Model Bakery   Cafe $
(📞707-963-8192; www.themodelbakery.com; 1357
Main St; dishes $5-10; ⏲6:30am-6pm Mon-Sat,
7am-5pm Sun) Good bakery with scones, muf-
fins, salads, pizzas, sandwiches and excep-
tional coffee.

Gott's Roadside   American $$
(📞707-963-3486; http://gotts.com; 933 Main St;
mains $10-15; ⏲7am-9pm, to 10pm May-Sep; 👶)
🌿 Wiggle your toes in the grass and feast
on quality burgers – of beef or ahi tuna –
plus Cobb salads and fish tacos at this
classic roadside drive-in, whose original
name, 'Taylor's Auto Refresher,' remains on
the sign. Avoid weekend waits by phoning
ahead or ordering online. There's another at
Oxbow Public Market (p84).

Cindy's Backstreet Kitchen   New American $$
(📞707-963-1200; www.cindysbackstreetkitchen.
com; 1327 Railroad Ave; mains $16-28; ⏲11:30am-
9:30pm) 🌿 The inviting retro-homey decor
complements the Cal-American comfort
food, such as avocado-and-papaya salad,
wood-fired duck, steak with French fries
and burgers. The bar makes mean mojitos.

Restaurant at Meadowood   Californian $$$
(📞707-967-1205; www.meadowood.com; 900 Meado-
wood Lane; 9-course menu $225; ⏲5:30-10pm
Mon-Sat) If you couldn't score reservations
at French Laundry (p87), fear not: Meadowood – the valley's only other Michelin-
three-star restaurant – has a slightly more
sensibly priced menu, elegantly unfussy
dining room, and lavish haute cuisine
that's not too esoteric. Auberge (p88) has

A LOVELY SPOT FOR A PICNIC

Unlike Sonoma, there aren't many
places to picnic legally in Napa.
Regusci (p33) and Lava Vine (p33)
allow it, but call ahead and remember
to buy a bottle (or glass, if available)
of your host's wine. If you don't finish
it, California law forbids driving with
an uncorked bottle in the car (keep it
in the trunk).

Napa Valley South

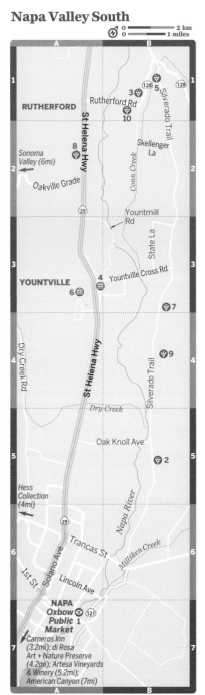

0 —— 2 km
0 —— 1 miles

Napa Valley South

◎ Sights

1	Darioush	B5
2	Frog's Leap	B1
3	Ma(i)sonry	A3
4	Mumm Napa	B1
5	Napa Valley Museum	A3
6	Oxbow Public Market	A7
7	Regusci	B3
8	Robert Mondavi	A2
9	Robert Sinskey	B4
10	Round Pond	B1

better views, but Meadowood's food and service far surpass it.

Terra   Californian $$$

(☑ 707-963-8931; www.terrarestaurant.com; 1345 Railroad Ave; 4-/5-/6-course menus $78/93/105; ◎ 6-9pm Wed-Sun) Seamlessly blending Japanese, French and Italian culinary styles, Terra is one of Wine Country's top tables – the signature is broiled sake-marinated black cod with shrimp dumplings in shiso broth. The adjoining bar serves small bites without reservations, but the dining room's the thing.

🛍 Shopping

Main St is lined with high-end boutiques (think $100 socks), but some mom-and-pop shops remain.

Woodhouse Chocolates   Food

(www.woodhousechocolate.com; 1367 Main St; ◎ 10:30am-5:30pm) Woodhouse looks more like Tiffany than a candy shop, with house-made chocolates similarly priced, but their quality is beyond reproach.

Napa Soap Company   Beauty

(www.napasoap.com; 651 Main St; ◎ 10am-5:30pm) 🌿 Eco-friendly, locally produced bath products.

Baksheesh   Homewares

(www.baksheeshfairtrade.com; 1327 Main St; ◎ 10am-6pm) 🌿 Handcrafted fair-trade home decor from 38 countries.

Lolo's Consignment   Vintage

(www.lolosconsignment.com; 1120 Main St; ◎ 10:30am-4pm Mon, to 5:30pm Tue-Sat, 11am-4pm Sun) Groovy cheap dresses and cast-off cashmere.

ⓘ Information

St Helena Welcome Center (☎707-963-4456; www.sthelena.com; 657 Main St; ⊙9am-5pm Mon-Fri, plus 10am-4pm Sat-Sun May-Nov) The visitor center has information and lodging assistance.

Calistoga & Around

Famed 19th-century author Robert Louis Stevenson said of Calistoga: 'the whole neighborhood of Mt St Helena is full of sulfur and boiling springs...Calistoga itself seems to repose on a mere film above a boiling, subterranean lake.'

The town's odd name comes from Sam Brannan, who founded Calistoga in 1859, believing it would develop like the New York spa town of Saratoga. Apparently Sam liked his drink and at the founding ceremony tripped on his tongue, proclaiming it the 'Cali-stoga' of 'Sara-fornia.' The name stuck.

- - - - - - - - - - - - - - - - - - - -

◉ Sights

Hwys 128 and 29 run together from Rutherford through St Helena; in Calistoga, they split. Hwy 29 turns east and becomes Lincoln Ave, continuing across Silverado Trail, toward Clear Lake. Hwy 128 continues north as Foothill Blvd (not St Helena Hwy). Calistoga's shops and restaurants line Lincoln Ave.

Sharpsteen Museum   Museum

(☎707-942-5911; www.sharpsteen-museum.org; 1311 Washington St; suggested donation $3; ⊙11am-4pm; ♿) **FREE** Across from the picturesque 1902 City Hall (originally an opera house), the Sharpsteen Museum was created by an ex-Disney animator (whose Oscar is on display) and houses a fantastic diorama of town in the 1860s, big Victorian dollhouse, full-size horse-drawn carriage, cool taxidermy and a restored cottage from Brannan's original resort. (The only Brannan cottage still at its original site is at 106 Wappo Ave).

Bale Grist Mill &
Bothe-Napa Valley State Parks   Historic Park

(☎707-942-4575; parks.ca.gov; ♿) Both these parks have picnic areas and admission to one includes the other. **Bale Grist Mill State Historic Park** (☎707-963-2236; adult/child $5/2; ♿) features a 36ft-high water-powered mill wheel dating to 1846 – the largest still operating in North America; Saturdays and Sundays (and sometimes Fridays and Mon-

days) from 10am to 4pm, it grinds flour. A mile-long trail leads to adjacent **Bothe-Napa Valley State Park** (☎707-942-4575; parking $8; ⊙8am-sunset; ♿), where there's a **swimming pool** ($5), and camping (p91), plus hiking through redwood groves.

If you're two or more adults, go first to Bothe and pay $8, instead of the per-head charge at Bale Grist. The mill and both parks are on Hwy 29/128, midway between St Helena and Calistoga. In early October, look for living-history festival **Old Mill Days.**

Old Faithful Geyser   Geyser
See page 31

Petrified Forest   Forest
See page 32

Safari West   Wildlife Reserve
See page 32

Robert Louis Stevenson State Park   Park
See page 33

- - - - - - - - - - - - - - - - - - - -

🏃 Activities

Oat Hill Mine Trail   Cycling, Hiking
One of Northern California's most technically challenging trails, OHM Trail draws hardcore mountain bikers and hikers. Softcore walkers, take heart: a moderately strenuous half-mile up from town, there's a bench with incredible valley views. The trailhead is at the intersection of Hwy 29 and Silverado Trail.

Calistoga Bike Shop   Bicycle Rental
(☎707-942-9687, 866-942-2453; www.calistogabike shop.com; 1318 Lincoln Ave; ⊙10am-6pm) Rents full-suspension mountain bikes ($75 per day) and hybrids ($12/39 per hour/day), and provides reliable trail information. Wine-touring packages ($90 per day) include wine-rack baskets and free wine pickup.

Spas
See page 32

- - - - - - - - - - - - - - - - - - - -

🛏 Sleeping

Bothe-Napa Valley State
Park Campground   Campground $
(☎800-444-7275; www.reserveamerica.com; 3801 Hwy 128; camping & RV sites $35; ♿🐾) Three miles south, Bothe has shady camping near redwoods, coin-operated showers,

INFO: SHIPPING

and gorgeous hiking (p91). Sites 28 to 36 are most secluded.

★ Mountain Home Ranch   Resort $$

(⟳ 707-942-6616; www.mountainhomeranch.com; 3400 Mountain Home Ranch Rd; r $111-121, cabins $71-156; @ 🛜 🞉) 🏊 In continuous operation since 1913, this 340-acre homestead outside town is a flashback to old California. Doubling as a retreat center, the ranch has simple lodge rooms and rustic freestanding cabins, some with kitchens and fireplaces, ideal for families, but you may be here during someone else's family reunion or spiritual quest.

No matter. With miles of oak-woodland trails, a hilltop swimming pool, private lake with canoeing and fishing, and a hike to warm springs in a magical fault-line canyon, you may hardly notice – and you may never make it to a single winery. Breakfast is included, but you'll have to drive 15 minutes to town for dinner. Pack hiking boots, not high heels.

Dr Wilkinson's Motel & Hideaway Cottages   Motel, Cottages $$

(⟳ 707-942-4102; www.drwilkinson.com; 1507 Lincoln Ave; r $149-255, cottages $165-270; 🞉 @ 🛜 🞉) This good-value vintage-1950s motel has well-kept rooms facing a swimming-pool courtyard with hot tub, three pools (one indoors), and mud baths. Also rents simple, great-value stand-alone cottages with kitchens at the affiliated Hideaway Cottages, also with pool and hot tub.

Solage   Resort $$$

(⟳ 866-942-7442, 707-226-0800; www.solagecalistoga.com; 755 Silverado Trail; r $530-675; 🞉 🛜 🞉 🞉) 🏊 Calistoga's top spa-hotel ups the style factor, with Cali-chic semidetached cottages and a glam palm-tree-lined pool. Rooms are austere, with vaulted ceilings, zillion-thread-count linens and pebble-floor showers. Cruiser bikes included.

Indian Springs Resort   Resort $$$

(⟳ 707-942-4913; www.indianspringscalistoga.com; 1712 Lincoln Ave; lodge r $229-359, cottage $259-429, 2-bedroom cottage $359-499; 🞉 🛜 🞉) The definitive old-school Calistoga resort, Indian Springs has cottages facing a central lawn with palm trees, shuffleboard, bocce, hammocks and Weber grills – not unlike a vintage Florida resort. Some sleep six. There are also top-end, motel-style lodge rooms (adults only). Huge hot-springs-fed swimming pool.

Chateau De Vie   B&B $$$

(⟳ 877-558-2513, 707-942-6446; www.cdvnapavalley.com; 3250 Hwy 128; r incl breakfast $229-429; 🞉 🛜 🞉 🞉) Surrounded by vineyards, with gorgeous views of Mt St Helena, CDV has five modern, elegantly decorated B&B rooms with top-end amenities and zero froufrou. Charming owners serve wine on the sun-dappled patio, then leave you alone. Hot tub, big pool. Gay-friendly.

Meadowlark Country House   B&B $$$

(⟳ 800-942-5651, 707-942-5651; www.meadowlarkinn.com; 601 Petrified Forest Rd; r incl breakfast $210-265, ste $285; 🞉 🛜 🞉 🞉) On 20 acres west of town, Meadowlark has homey rooms decorated in contemporary style, most with decks and Jacuzzis. Outside there's a hot tub, sauna and clothing-optional pool. The truth-telling innkeeper lives elsewhere, offers helpful advice, then vanishes when you want privacy. There's a fabulous cottage for $465. Gay-friendly.

✕ Eating

Buster's Southern BBQ   Barbecue $

(⟳ 707-942-5605; www.busterssouthernbbq.com; 1207 Foothill Blvd; dishes $8-12; ⊙10am-7:30pm Mon-Sat, 10:30am-6pm Sun; 🚗) The sheriff dines at this indoor-outdoor barbecue joint, which serves smoky ribs, chicken, tri-tip steak and burgers, but closes early at dinnertime. Beer and wine.

Calistoga Inn & Brewery
American $$

(📞707-942-4101; www.calistogainn.com; 1250 Lincoln Ave; lunch mains $11-15, dinner $15-30; ⊙11:30am-3pm & 5:30-9pm) Locals crowd the outdoor beer garden Sundays. Midweek we prefer the country dining room's big oakwood tables – a homey spot for simple American cooking. Live music summer weekends.

Solbar
Californian $$$

(📞707-226-0850; www.solagecalistoga.com; 755 Silverado Trail; lunch mains $17-20, dinner $24-34; ⊙7am-11am, 11:30am-3pm & 5:30-9pm) 🌿 We like the spartan ag-chic look of this Michelin-starred resort restaurant, whose menu maximizes seasonal produce in elegant dishes, playfully composed. And this being a spa (p32), too, the menu is split for calorie-counters into light and hearty dishes. Reservations essential.

🍷 Drinking & Nightlife

Yo El Rey
Cafe

(📞707-942-1180; www.yoelreyroasting.com; 1217 Washington St; ⊙6:30am-6pm) 🌿 Hip kids favor this micro-roastery, which serves stellar small-batch, fair-trade coffee.

Hydro Grill
Bar

(📞707-942-9777; 1403 Lincoln Ave; ⊙8:30am-midnight Sun-Thu, to 2am Fri & Sat) Live music plays weekend evenings at this hoppin' corner bar-restaurant.

Solbar
Bar

(📞707-226-0850; www.solagecalistoga.com; 755 Silverado Trail; ⊙11am-9pm) Sip craft cocktails beside outdoor fireplaces and a palm-lined pool at this swank resort bar.

🛍 Shopping

Calistoga Pottery
Ceramics

(📞707-942-0216; www.calistogapottery.com; 1001 Foothill Blvd; ⊙9am-5pm) Artisanal pottery, hand-thrown on site.

Coperfield's Bookshop
Books

(📞707-942-1616; 1330 Lincoln Ave; ⊙10am-7pm Mon-Sat, 10am-6pm Sun) Indie bookshop, with local maps and guides.

ℹ Information

Chamber of Commerce & Visitors Center
(📞707-942-6333, 866-306-5588; www.calistogavisitors.com; 1133 Washington St; ⊙9am-5pm)

SONOMA VALLEY

(See page 36) Halfway up-valley, tiny Glen Ellen is straight from a Norman Rockwell painting – in stark contrast to the valley's northernmost town, Santa Rosa, the workaday urban center best known for traffic. If you have more than a day, explore Sonoma's quiet, rustic western side, along the Russian River Valley, and continue to the sea.

Sonoma Hwy/Hwy 12 is lined with wineries, and runs from Sonoma to Santa Rosa, to western Sonoma County; Arnold Dr has less traffic (but few wineries) and runs parallel, up the valley's western side, to Glen Ellen.

Sonoma Valley Wineries

Rolling grass-covered hills rise from 17-mile-long Sonoma Valley. Its 40-some wineries get less attention than Napa's, but many are equally good. If you love Zinfandel and Syrah, you're in for a treat.

Picnicking is allowed at Sonoma wineries. Get maps and discount coupons in the town of Sonoma or, if you're approaching from the south, the Sonoma Valley Visitors Bureau at Cornerstone Sonoma.

Plan at least five hours to visit the valley from bottom to top.

FLYING & BALLOONING

Wine Country is stunning from the air – a multihued tapestry of undulating hills, deep valleys and rambling vineyards. Make reservations.

The **Vintage Aircraft Company** (📞707-938-2444; www.vintageaircraft.com; 23982 Arnold Dr, Sonoma) flies over Sonoma in a vintage biplane with an awesome pilot who'll do loop-de-loops on request (add $50). Twenty-minute tours cost $175/260 for one/two adults.

Napa Valley's signature hot-air balloon flights leave around 6am or 7am, when the air is coolest; they usually include a champagne breakfast on landing. Adults pay about $200 to $250, and kids $150 to $175. Call **Balloons above the Valley** (📞800-464-6824, 707-253-2222; www.balloonrides.com) or **Napa Valley Balloons** (📞800-253-2224, 707-944-0228; www.napavalleyballoons.com), both in Yountville.

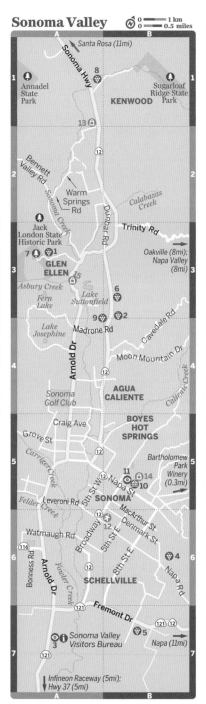

Sonoma Valley

0 — 1 km
0 — 0.5 miles

Sonoma Valley

◎ Sights

1	Benziger............................	A3
2	BR Cohn............................	B3
3	Cornerstone Sonoma...............	A7
4	Gundlach-Bundschu Winery.........	B6
5	Homewood	B7
6	Imagery Estate....................	B3
7	Jack London State Historic Park.....	A3
8	Kaz	A1
9	Little Vineyards	A4
10	Mission San Francisco Solano de Sonoma	B5
11	Sonoma Barracks	B5

⊕ Activities, Courses & Tours

12	Traintown	B6

🛍 Shopping

13	Figone's Olive Oil	A1
14	Vella Cheese Co...................	B5
15	Wine Country Chocolates Tasting Bar	A3

Homewood Winery
See page 37

Gundlach-Bundschu Winery
See page 37

Bartholomew Park Winery
See page 40

Little Vineyards Winery
See page 22

BR Cohn Winery
See page 22

Imagery Estate Winery
See page 38

Benziger Winery
See page 39

Kaz Winery
See page 40

SONOMA & AROUND

Fancy boutiques may be replacing hardware stores lately, but Sonoma still retains an old-fashioned charm, thanks to the plaza and its surrounding frozen-in-time historic buildings. You can legally drink on the plaza – a rarity in California parks – but only between 11:30am and sunset.

Sonoma Hwy (Hwy 12) runs through town. Sonoma Plaza, laid out by General Vallejo in 1834, is the heart of downtown, lined with hotels, restaurants, tasting rooms and shops. The visitors bureau has a walking-tour brochure. Immediately north along Hwy 12, expect a brief suburban landscape before the valley's pastoral gorgeousness begins.

⊙ Sights

★ Sonoma Plaza
Square

(btwn Napa, Spain & 1st Sts) Smack in the center of the plaza, the Mission-revival-style city hall, built between 1906 and 1908, has identical facades on four sides, reportedly because plaza businesses all demanded City Hall face their direction. At the plaza's northeast corner, the Bear Flag Monument marks Sonoma's moment of revolutionary glory. The weekly farmers market (5:30pm to 8pm Tuesday, April to October) showcases Sonoma's incredible produce.

Sonoma State Historic Park
Historic Site
See page 37

La Haye Art Center
Arts Center
(🖉 707-996-9665; 148 E Napa St; ⊙11am-5pm) FREE At this collective in a converted foundry, you can tour a storefront gallery and meet the artists – sculptor, potter and painters – in their studios.

Sonoma Valley Museum of Art
Museum
(🖉 707-939-7862; www.svma.org; 551 Broadway; adult/family $5/8; ⊙11am-5pm Wed-Sun) Though this museum presents compelling work by local and international artists, such as David Hockney, the annual standout is October's Día de los Muertos exhibition.

Cornerstone Sonoma
Gardens
See page 37

🏃 Activities
Many local inns provide bicycles.

Traintown
Amusement Park
See page 36

Sonoma Valley Cyclery
Bicycle Rental
(🖉 707-935-3377; www.sonomacyclery.com; 20091 Broadway/Hwy 12; bikes per day from $30; ⊙10am-6pm Mon-Sat, to 4pm Sun; 📶) Sonoma is ideal for cycling – not too hilly – with multiple wineries near downtown. Book ahead for weekends.

Willow Stream Spa at Sonoma Mission Inn
Spa
(🖉 707-938-9000; www.fairmont.com/sonoma; 100 Boyes Blvd; ⊙7:30am-8pm) Few Wine Country spas compare with glitzy Sonoma Mission Inn, where two treatments on the weekend – or $89 on a weekday (make reservations) – allow use of three outdoor and two indoor mineral pools, gym, sauna, and herbal steam room at the Romanesque bathhouse. No under 18s.

⚑ Courses

Ramekins Sonoma Valley Culinary School
Cooking Course
(🖉 707-933-0450; www.ramekins.com; 450 W Spain St; 📶) Offers demonstrations and hands-on classes for home chefs. Also runs weekend 'culinary camps' for adults and kids.

🛏 Sleeping
Off-season rates plummet. Reserve ahead. Ask about parking; some historic inns have no lots. Also consider Glen Ellen and, if counting pennies, Santa Rosa.

Sonoma Chalet
B&B $$
(🖉 800-938-3129, 707-938-3129; www.sonomachalet.com; 18935 5th St W; r $160-180, with shared bath $140, cottages $195-225) A historic farmstead surrounded by rolling hills, Sonoma Chalet has rooms in a Swiss chalet–style house adorned with little balconies and country-style bric-a-brac. We love the free-standing cottages; Laura's has a wood-burning fireplace. All rooms come with breakfast, which is served on a deck overlooking a nature preserve. No air-con in rooms with shared bath. No phones, no internet.

Sonoma Hotel
Historic Hotel $$
(🖉 800-468-6016, 707-996-2996; www.sonomahotel.com; 110 W Spain St; r incl breakfast $170-200, ste $250; ❄🖉) Long on charm, this good-value, vintage-1880s hotel, decorated with country-style willow-wood furnishings, sits right on the plaza. Double-pane glass blocks the noise, but there's no elevator or parking lot.

Swiss Hotel
Historic Hotel $$
(🖉 707-938-2884; www.swisshotelsonoma.com; 18 W Spain St; r incl breakfast Mon-Fri $150-170, Sat & Sun $200-240; ❄🖉) It opened in 1905, so you'll forgive the wavy floors. The floral prints are

Sonoma State Historic Park

likewise dated, but rooms are large, good value and share a plaza-view balcony. Downstairs there's a raucous bar and restaurant. No parking lot or elevator.

El Dorado Hotel
Boutique Hotel $$$

(☎707-996-3220; www.eldoradosonoma.com; 405 1st St W; r Mon-Fri $165-265, Sat & Sun $245-325; P❋@🖥🏊) Stylish touches, such as high-end linens, justify rates and compensate for the rooms' compact size, as do private balconies, which overlook the plaza or rear courtyard (we prefer the plaza view, despite noise). No elevator.

El Pueblo Inn
Motel $$$

(☎707-996-3651, 800-900-8844; www. elpuebloinn.com; 896 W Napa St; r incl breakfast $189-239; ❋@🖥🏊) One mile west of downtown, family-owned El Pueblo has surprisingly cushy rooms with great beds. The big lawns and the heated pool are perfect for kids; parents appreciate the 24-hour hot tub.

Sonoma's Best Guest Cottages
Cottages $$$

(☎800-291-8962, 707-933-0340; www. sonomasbestcottages.com; 1190 E Napa St; cottages $199-349, q $279-395; ❋🖥) Each of these four colorful, inviting cottages has a bedroom, living room, kitchen and barbecue, with comfy furniture, stereos, DVDs and bicycles. One mile east of the plaza.

🍴 Eating

There's creek-side picnicking, with barbecue grills, up-valley at Sugarloaf Ridge State Park (p98). Find late-night taco trucks on Hwy 12, between Boyes Blvd and Aqua Caliente.

Angelo's Wine Country Deli
Deli $

(☎707-938-3688; 23400 Arnold Dr; sandwiches $7; ⊙9am-5:30pm) Look for the cow on the roof of this roadside deli, south of town, a fave for fat sandwiches and homemade jerky. In springtime, little lambs graze outside.

Pearl's Diner
Diner $

(☎707-996-1783; 561 5th St W; mains $7-10; ⊙7am-2:30pm; 🚻) Across from Safeway's west-facing wall, greasy-spoon Pearl's serves giant American breakfasts, including standout bacon and waffles with batter enriched by melted vanilla ice cream.

★Fremont Diner
American $$

(☎707-938-7370; http://thefremontdiner.com; 2698 Fremont Dr; mains $10-16; ⊙8am-3pm Mon-Wed, to 9pm Thu-Sun; 🚻) ✎ Lines snake out the door peak times at this farm-to-table roadside diner. We prefer the indoor tables, but will happily accept a picnic table in the big outdoor tent to feast on ricotta pancakes with real maple syrup, chicken and waffles, oyster po' boys, finger-licking barbecue and skillet-baked cornbread. Arrive early, or late, to beat queues.

Sunflower Caffé & Wine Bar
Cafe $$

(707-996-6845; www.sonomasunflower.com; 421 1st St W; dishes $8-15; 7am-4pm;) The big back garden at this local hangout is a great spot for breakfast, a no-fuss lunch or afternoon wine.

Red Grape
Italian $$

(707-996-4103; http://theredgrape.com; 529 1st St W; mains $10-20; 11:30am-10pm;) A reliable spot for an easy meal, Red Grape serves good thin-crust pizzas and big salads in a cavernous, echoey space. Good for takeout, too.

★ Cafe La Haye
Californian $$$

(707-935-5994; www.cafelahaye.com; 140 E Napa St; mains $20-32; 5:30-9pm Tue-Sat) One of Sonoma's top tables for earthy New American cooking, La Haye only uses produce sourced from within 60 miles. Its dining room gets packed cheek-by-jowl and service can border on perfunctory, but the clean simplicity and flavor-packed cooking make it many foodies' first choice. Reserve well ahead.

The Girl & the Fig
French $$$

(707-938-3634; www.thegirlandthefig.com; 11 W Spain St; mains $20-27; 11:30am-10pm Mon-Fri, 11am-11pm Sat, 10am-10pm Sun) For a festive evening, book a garden table at this French-provincial bistro, with good small plates ($12 to $14) including steamed mussels with matchstick fries, and duck confit with lentils. Weekday three-course prix-fixe costs $36, add $12 for wine. Stellar cheeses. Reservations essential.

🍷 Drinking & Entertainment

Free jazz concerts happen on the plaza every second Tuesday, June to September, 6pm to 8:30pm; arrive early, bring a picnic.

Murphy's Irish Pub
Pub

(707-935-0660; www.sonomapub.com; 464 1st E; noon-11pm) Don't ask for Bud – there're only *real* brews here. Good hand-cut fries and shepherd's pie, too. Live music Thursday through Sunday evenings.

Swiss Hotel
Bar

(www.swisshotelsonoma.com; 18 W Spain St; 11:30am-midnight) Locals and tourists crowd the 1909 Swiss Hotel for cocktails. There's OK food, but the bar's the thing.

Hopmonk Tavern
Brewery

(707-935-9100; www.hopmonk.com; 691 Broadway; 11:30am-10pm) This happening gastro-pub (dishes $10 to $20) and beer garden takes its brews seriously, with 16 on tap, served in type-appropriate glassware. Live music Friday through Sunday.

Sebastiani Theatre
Cinema

(707-996-2020; sebastianitheatre.com; 476 1st St E) The plaza's gorgeous 1934 Mission-revival cinema screens art-house and revival films, and sometimes live theater.

🛍 Shopping

Vella Cheese Co
Food

See page 38

Tiddle E Winks
Toys

(707-939-6933; www.tiddleewinks.com; 115 E Napa St; 10:30am-5:30pm Mon-Sat, 11am-5pm Sun;) Vintage five-and-dime, with classic, mid-20th-century toys.

Sign of the Bear
Homewares

(707-996-3722; 435 1st St W; 10am-6pm) Kitchen-gadget freaks, make a beeline to this indie cookware store.

ℹ Information

Sonoma Post Office (800-275-8777; www.usps.com; 617 Broadway; 9am-5pm Mon-Fri)
Sonoma Valley Hospital (707-935-5000; www.svh.com; 347 Andrieux St) Twenty-four-hour emergency room.
Sonoma Valley Visitors Bureau (707-996-1090; www.sonomavalley.com; 453 1st E; 9am-5pm Mon-Sat, 10am-5pm Sun) Arranges accommodations; has a good walking-tour pamphlet and events information. There's another at Cornerstone Sonoma (p37).

Glen Ellen & Kenwood

Sleepy Glen Ellen is a snapshot of old Sonoma, with white-picket fences and tiny cottages beside a poplar-lined creek. When downtown Sonoma is jammed, you can wander quiet Glen Ellen and feel far away. It's ideal for a leg-stretching stopover between wineries or a romantic overnight – the nighttime sky blazes with stars. Arnold Dr is the main drag and the valley's backway route. Kenwood lies just north, along Hwy 12, but has no town center like Glen Ellen's. For services, drive 8 miles south to Sonoma. Glen Ellen's biggest draws are Jack London State Historic Park and Benziger winery (p39).

TOURING NAPA & SONOMA WINE COUNTRY

You have the most flexibility by driving your own vehicle, but to drink and not drive, here are some tour options. Note that some wineries do not allow limousines (because the people in them are often obnoxious and don't buy anything); and limousine companies have set itineraries with little flexibility (ie, you'll have few choices about which wineries you visit).

Bicycle Tours & Rentals

Guided tours start around $90 per day including bikes, tastings and lunch. Daily rentals cost $25 to $85; make reservations.

Backroads (☎800-462-2848; www.backroads.com) All-inclusive guided biking and walking.

Calistoga Bike Shop (☎707-942-9687; www.calistogabikeshop.com; 1318 Lincoln Ave, Calistoga; ⊙10am-6pm) Wine-tour rental package ($90) includes wine pickup.

Getaway Adventures (☎800-499-2453, 707-568-3040; http://getawayadventures.com; tours $149) Great guided tours, some combined with kayaking, of Napa, Sonoma, Calistoga, Healdsburg and Russian River. Single- and multiday trips.

Other Tours

Wine Country Jeep Tours (☎800-539-5337, 707-546-1822; www.jeeptours.com; 3hr tour $75) Tour Wine Country's back roads and boutique wineries by Jeep, year-round at 10am and 1pm. Also operates tours of Sonoma Coast.

Antique Tours Limousine (☎707-761-3949; www.antiquetours.net) Drive in style in a 1947 Packard convertible; tours cost $120 to $170 per hour.

Beau Wine Tours (☎800-387-2328, 707-938-8001; www.beauwinetours.com) Winery tours in sedans and stretch limos; charges $60 to $95 per hour (four- to six-hour minimum).

◉ Sights & Activities

Jack London State Historic Park   Hiking
See page 39

Sugarloaf Ridge State Park   Hiking
(☎707-833-5712; www.parks.ca.gov; 2605 Adobe Canyon Rd, Kenwood; per car $8) There's fantastic hiking – when it's not blazingly hot. On clear days, Bald Mountain has drop-dead views to the sea; Bushy Peak Trail peers into Napa Valley. Both are moderately strenuous; plan four hours round-trip.

Morton's Warm Springs   Swimming
(☎707-833-5511; www.mortonswarmsprings.com; 1651 Warm Springs Rd, Glen Ellen; adult/child $15/5; ⊙10am-6pm Sat, Sun & holidays May & Sep, Tue-Sun Jun-Aug; ⊞) This old-fashioned family swim club has two mineral pools, limited hiking, volleyball and BBQ facilities. No credit cards Tuesday to Friday: exact change required. From Sonoma Hwy in Kenwood, turn west on Warm Springs Rd.

Triple Creek Horse Outfit   Horseback Riding
(☎707-887-8700; www.triplecreekhorseoutfit.com; 60/90min rides $75/95; ⊙Wed-Mon) Explore Jack London State Park by horseback for stunning vistas over Sonoma Valley. Reservations required.

⊨ Sleeping

Sugarloaf Ridge State Park   Campground $
(☎800-444-7275; www.reserveamerica.com; 2605 Adobe Canyon Rd, Kenwood; tent & RV sites $35; ⊞) Sonoma's nearest camping is north of Kenwood at this lovely hilltop park, with 50 drive-in sites, clean coin-operated showers and great hiking.

Jack London Lodge   Motel $$
(☎707-938-8510; www.jacklondonlodge.com; 13740 Arnold Dr, Glen Ellen; r Mon-Fri $124, Sat & Sun $189; ❋ 🜨 ⊞) An old-fashioned wood-sided motel, with well-kept rooms decorated with antique repros, this is a weekday bargain – and the manager will sometimes negotiate rates. Outside there's a hot tub; next door, a saloon.

Glen Ellen Cottages
Bungalow $$

(📞707-996-1174; www.glenelleninn.com; 13670 Arnold Dr, Glen Ellen; cottage Mon-Fri $139-159, Sat & Sun $209-249; 🎂🎐) Hidden behind Glen Ellen Inn, these five creek-side cottages are designed for romance, with oversized jetted tubs, steam showers and gas fireplaces.

★ Beltane Ranch
B&B $$$

(📞707-996-6501; www.beltaneranch.com; 11775 Hwy 12, Glen Ellen; d incl breakfast $160-285; 🎐) 🍴 Surrounded by horse pastures and vineyards, Beltane is a throwback to 19th-century Sonoma. The cheerful, lemon-yellow, 1890s ranch house has double porches, lined with swinging chairs and white wicker. Though it's technically a B&B, each country-Americana-style room has a private entrance – nobody will make you pet the cat. Breakfast in bed. No phones or TVs mean zero distraction from pastoral bliss.

Gaige House Inn
B&B $$$

(📞707-935-0237, 800-935-0237; www.gaige. com; 13540 Arnold Dr, Glen Ellen; d incl breakfast from $275, ste from $425; 🎐🎐🎂🎐) Among the valley's most chic inns, Gaige has 23 rooms, five inside an 1890 house decked out in Euro-Asian style. Best are the Japanese-style 'Zen suites,' with requisite high-end bells and whistles, including freestanding tubs made from hollowed-out granite boulders. Fabulous.

✕ Eating

Glen Ellen Village Market
Deli, Market $

(www.sonoma-glenellenmkt.com; 13751 Arnold Dr, Glen Ellen; 🕐6am-8pm) Fantastic market with huge deli, ideal for picnickers.

Garden Court Cafe
Cafe $

(📞707-935-1565; www.gardencourtcafe.com; 13647 Arnold Dr, Glen Ellen; mains $9-12; 🕐8:30am-2pm Wed-Mon) Basic breakfasts, sandwiches and salads.

Fig Cafe & Winebar
French, Californian $$

(📞707-938-2130; www.thefigcafe.com; 13690 Arnold Dr, Glen Ellen; mains $18-22; 🕐10am-3pm Sat & Sun, 5:30-9pm daily) The Fig's earthy California–Provençal comfort food includes flash-fried calamari with spicy lemon aioli, duck confit and *moules-frites* (mussels and French fries). Good wine prices and weekend brunch give reason to return.

Yeti
Indian $$

(📞707-996-9930; www.yetirestaurant.com; 14301 Arnold Dr, Glen Ellen; mains $12-22; 🕐11:30am-2:30pm & 5-9pm) Surprisingly good Indian and Nepalese cooking, served on a creek-side patio at a converted mill, make Yeti worth seeking out. Great value.

Kenwood Restaurant & Bar
Californian $$$

(📞707-833-6326; www.kenwoodrestaurant.com; 9900 Sonoma Hwy, Kenwood; mains $22-30; 🕐11:30am-8:30pm Wed-Sun) 🍴 A stone patio flanks vineyards and flowering gardens at this roadhouse restaurant, lovely for a lingering lunch. The chef showcases quality ingredients by local producers in simple delicious dishes like pork chops with bacon or roasted chicken. The small-plates menu ($10 to $16) is ideal for a quick bite between wineries. Reservations advised.

Aventine
Italian $$$

(📞707-934-8911; http://glenellen.aventinehospitality. com; 14301 Arnold Dr, Glen Ellen; mains $14-28; 🕐4:30-10pm Tue-Fri, 11am-10pm Sat & Sun) The Sonoma outpost of the popular San Francisco and Hollywood restaurants occupies an atmospheric former grist mill with a sun-dappled outdoor patio, and serves Italian-derived dishes, including mozzarella-stuffed meatballs with pesto over polenta. Make reservations.

🛍 Shopping

Wine Country Chocolates Tasting Bar
Food

See page 39

Figone's Olive Oil
Food

See page 40

RUSSIAN RIVER AREA

The Russian River begins in the mountains north of Ukiah, in Mendocino County, but the most-known sections lie southwest of Healdsburg, where the river cuts a serpentine course toward the sea. Just north of Santa Rosa, River Rd, the lower valley's main artery, connects Hwy 101 with coastal Hwy 1 at Jenner. Hwy 116 heads northwest from Cotati through Sebastopol, then at Guerneville joins River Rd and cuts west to the sea. Westside Rd connects Guerneville and Healdsburg. West County's winding roads get confusing and there's limited cell service; carry a proper map.

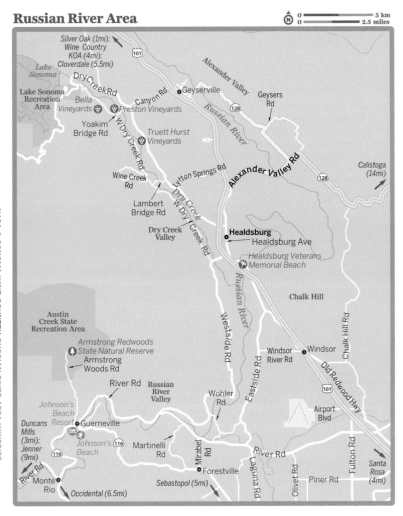

Russian River Area Wineries

Sonoma County's wine-growing regions encompass several diverse areas, each famous for different reasons. Pick up the free, useful *Russian River Wine Road* map (www.wineroad.com) in tourist-brochure racks.

Russian River Valley

Nighttime coastal fog drifts up the Russian River Valley, then usually clears by midday. Pinot Noir does beautifully, as does Chardonnay, which also grows in hotter regions, but prefers the longer 'hang time' of cooler climes. The highest concentration of wineries is along Westside Rd, between Guerneville and Healdsburg.

Hartford Family Winery   Winery

(☎ 707-887-8030; www.hartfordwines.com; 8075 Martinelli Rd, Forestville; tasting $15; ⏱ 10am-4:30pm) 🍃 Surprisingly upscale for West County, Hartford sits in a pastoral valley surrounded by redwood-forested hills, on one of the area's prettiest back roads. It specializes in fine single-vineyard Pinot (12 kinds),

Chardonnay and Zinfandel from old-vine fruit. Umbrella-shaded picnic tables dot the garden. Bottles are $38 to $90 and the tasting fee is waived with purchase.

Korbel
Winery

See page 47

Iron Horse Vineyards
Winery

(☑ 707-887-1507; www.ironhorsevineyards.com; 9786 Ross Station Rd, Sebastopol; tasting $20; ☺ 10am-4:30pm) Atop a hill with drop-dead views over the county, Iron Horse is known for Pinot Noir and sparkling wines, which the White House often pours. The outdoor tasting room is refreshingly unfussy; when you're done with your wine, pour it in the grass. Sunday noon to 4pm, April to October, they serve oysters ($3). Located off Hwy 116. Bottles cost $27 to $85.

Marimar
Winery

(☑ 707-823-4365; www.marimarestate.com; 11400 Graton Rd, Sebastopol; tasting $10-15; ☺ 11am-4pm; ⚉) ✎ Middle-of-nowhere Marimar specializes in all-organic Pinot – seven different kinds – and Spanish varietals. The hacienda-style hilltop tasting room has a knockout vineyard-view terrace, good for picnics. Also consider tapas-and-wine pairings ($45). Bottles are $29 to $57.

Gary Farrell
Winery

(☑ 707-473-2900; www.garyfarrellwines.com; 10701 Westside Rd, Healdsburg; tasting $15-25; ☺ 10:30am-4:30pm) High on a hilltop, overlooking the Russian River, Gary Farrell's tasting room sits perched among second-growth redwoods. The elegant Chardonnay and long-finish Pinot, made by a big-name winemaker, score high marks for consistency. Bottles are $32 to $60.

Dry Creek Valley

West of Hwy 101, between Healdsburg and Lake Sonoma. Dry Creek Rd is the fast-moving main thoroughfare. Parallel-running West Dry Creek Rd is an undulating country lane with no center stripe – one of Sonoma's great back roads, ideal for cycling.

Quivira
Winery

(☑ 707-431-8333; www.quivirawine.com; 4900 West Dry Creek Rd; tasting $10; ☺ 11am-5pm; ♿ ⚉) ✎ Sunflowers, lavender and crowing roosters greet you at this winery and biodynamic farm, with self-guided garden tours and a picnic grove beside the vines. Kids can giggle with

pigs and chickens, while you sample Rhône varietals, unusual blends, and lip-smacking Sauvignon Blanc. Bottles are $22 to $45; the tasting fee is refundable with purchase.

Unti Vineyards
Winery

(☑ 707-433-5590; www.untivineyards.com; 4202 Dry Creek Rd; tasting $5; ☺ by appointment 10am-4pm; ⚉) ✎ Inside a vineyard-view tasting room, Unti pours all estate-grown reds – including Châteauneuf-du-Pape–style Grenache, compelling Syrah, and superb Sangiovese – favored by oenophiles for their structured tannins and concentrated fruit. If you love small-batch wines, don't miss Unti. Bottles are $23 to $40 and the tasting fee is refundable with a purchase.

Family Wineries
Winery

(☑ 707-433-0100; familywines.com; 4791 Dry Creek Rd; tasting $10; ☺ 10:30am-4:30pm) Sample multiple varietals at this cooperative, which showcases six boutique wineries too small to have their own tasting rooms. Tasting fee is refundable with a purchase.

Truett Hurst Vineyards
Winery

See page 43

Bella Vineyards
Winery

See page 43

Preston Vineyards
Winery

See page 43

Alexander Valley

Bucolic Alexander Valley flanks the Mayacamas Mountains, with postcard-perfect vistas and wide-open vineyards. Summers are hot, ideal for Cabernet Sauvignon, Merlot and warm-weather Chardonnays, but there's also fine Sauvignon Blanc and Zinfandel. For events info, visit www.alexandervalley.org.

Hanna
Winery

(☑ 800-854-3987, 707-431-4310; http://hannawinery.com; 9280 Hwy 128, Healdsburg; tasting $10-20; ☺ 10am-4pm; ⚉) Abutting oak-studded hills, Hanna's tasting room has lovely vineyard views and good picnicking. At the bar, find estate-grown Merlot and Cabernet, and big-fruit Zins and Syrah. Sit-down wine-and-cheese tastings are available ($25). Bottles cost $18 to $56.

Hawkes
Tasting Room

(☑ 707-433-4295; www.hawkeswine.com; 6734 Hwy 128, Healdsburg; tasting $10; ☺ 10am-5pm; ⚉)

WINE TASTING

The best way to discover the real Wine Country is to avoid factory wineries and visit family-owned boutique houses (producing fewer than 20,000 annual cases) and mid-sized houses (20,000 to 60,000 annual cases). Why does it matter? Think of it. If you were to attend two dinner parties, one for 10 people, one for 1000, which would have the better food? Small wineries maintain tighter control. Also, you won't easily find these wines elsewhere.

Tastings are called 'flights' and include four to six different wines. Napa wineries charge $10 to $50. In Sonoma Valley, tastings cost $5 to $20, often refundable with purchase. In Sonoma County, tastings are free or $5 to $10. You must be 21 to taste.

Do not drink and drive. The curvy roads are dangerous, and police monitor traffic, especially on Napa's Hwy 29.

To avoid burnout, visit no more than three wineries per day. Most open daily from 10am or 11am to 4pm or 5pm, but call ahead if your heart's set, or you absolutely want a tour, especially in Napa, where law requires that some wineries accept visitors only by appointment. If you're buying, ask if there's a wine club, which is free to join and provides discounts, but you'll have to agree to buy a certain amount annually.

Friendly Hawkes makes an easy stopover while you're exploring the valley. The single-vineyard Cab is damn good, as is the blend; there's also a clean-and-crisp, non-malolactic Chardonnay. Bottles are $30 to $70 and the tasting fee is refundable with a purchase.

Stryker Sonoma   Winery

(✆ 707-433-1944; www.strykersonoma.com; 5110 Hwy 128, Geyserville; tasting $10; ⊙ 10:30am-5pm; 🐾) 🍷 Wow, what a view from the hilltop concrete-and-glass tasting room at Stryker Sonoma. The standouts are fruit-forward Zinfandel and Sangiovese, which you can't buy anywhere else. Good picnicking. Bottles are $20 to $50; tasting fee is refundable with purchase.

Trentadue   Winery

(✆ 888-332-3032, 707-433-3104; www.trentadue. com; 19170 Geyserville Ave, Geyserville; tasting $5-10; ⊙ 10am-5pm; 🐾) Specializes in ports (ruby, not tawny); the chocolate port makes a great gift.

Sebastopol

This is the refreshingly unfussy side of Wine Country, and makes a good-value base for exploring the area.

Hwy 116 splits downtown; southbound traffic uses Main St, northbound traffic Petaluma Ave. North of town, it's called Gravenstein Hwy N and continues toward Guerneville; south of downtown, it's Gravenstein Hwy S, which heads toward Hwy 101 and Sonoma.

◉ Sights

Around Sebastopol, look for family-friendly farms, gardens, animal sanctuaries and pick-your-own orchards. For a countywide list, check out the Sonoma County Farm Trails Guide (www.farmtrails.org).

★ The Barlow   Market

(✆ 707-824-5600; thebarlow.net; 6770 McKinley St; ⊙ 8:30am-9:30pm; ♿) The Barlow occupies a former apple processing plant, covering 12 acres, re-purposed into a village of food producers, artists, winemakers, coffee roasters, spirits distillers and indie restaurateurs, who showcase West County's culinary and artistic diversity. Wander shed to shed, sample everything from house-brewed beer to nitrogen flash-frozen ice cream, and meet artisanal producers in their workshops. Thursdays 4pm to 8pm, mid-June to mid-October, the Barlow hosts a 'street fair,' with live music and local vendors.

Spirit Works Distillery   Distillery

(✆ 707-634-4793; www.spiritworksdistillery.com; 6790 McKinley St, 100, The Barlow; tasting $5, tour $15; ⊙ 11am-4pm Thu-Sun) 🍷 A bracing alternative to wine-tasting, Spirit Works crafts superb small-batch spirits – vodka, gin, sloe gin and (soon) whiskey – of organic California red-winter wheat. Sample and buy in the warehouse. Tours (by reservation) happen Friday to Sunday at 4pm. Bottles are $27 to $36.

California Carnivores
Gardens

(☎707-824-0433; www.californiacarnivores.com; 2833 Old Gravenstein Hwy S; ⏰10am-4pm Thu-Mon) Even vegans can't help admiring these incredible carnivorous plants – the largest collection in the US – including specimens from around the globe.

Farmers Market
Market

(www.sebastopolfarmmarket.org; cnr Petaluma & McKinley Aves; ⏰10am-1:30pm Sun) Meets at the downtown plaza.

⚜ Festivals & Events

Apple Blossom Festival
Cultural

(appleblossomfest.com) Live music, food, drink, wine, a parade and exhibits in April.

Gravenstein Apple Fair
Food

(www.gravensteinapplefair.com) Arts, crafts, food, wines and brews, games, live entertainment and farm-life activities in August.

🛏 Sleeping

Staying in Sebastopol is convenient to Russian River Valley, the coast, and Sonoma Valley.

Sebastopol Inn
Motel $$

(☎800-653-1082, 707-829-2500; www.sebastopolinn.com; 6751 Sebastopol Ave; r $119-209; ✳🔊☒) We like this independent, *non*-cookie-cutter

motel for its quiet, off-street location, usually reasonable rates and good-looking if basic rooms. Outside are grassy areas for kids and a hot tub.

Fairfield Inn & Suites
Hotel $$

(☎800-465-4329, 707-829-6677; www.winecountryhi. com; 1101 Gravenstein Hwy S; r $134-249; ✳@🔊☒) Generic but modern, this hotel has little extras, such as in-room refrigerators and coffee makers, plus a hot tub.

🍴 Eating

Fiesta Market
Market $

(Pacific Market; ☎707-823-9735; fiestamkt.com; 550 Gravenstein Hwy N; ⏰8am-8pm) Excellent for groceries and picnics; north of downtown.

East-West Cafe
Mediterranean $

(☎707-829-2822; www.eastwestcafesebastopol. com; 128 N Main St; meals $9-13; ⏰8am-9pm Mon-Sat, to 8pm Sun; 🥡🚸) 🍃 This unfussy cafe serves everything from grass-fed burgers to macrobiotic wraps, stir-fries to *huevos rancheros* (corn tortilla with fried egg and chili-tomato sauce). Good blue-corn pancakes at breakfast.

Screamin' Mimi
Ice Cream $

(☎707-823-5902; www.screaminmimisicecream.com; 6902 Sebastopol Ave; ⏰11am-10pm) Delish homemade ice cream.

JUDY BELLAH/GETTY IMAGES ©

Forchetta Bastoni
Italian, Southeast Asian $$

(☑707-829-9500; www.forchettabastoni.com; 6948 Sebastopol Ave; mains $10-16; ⊙11am-9pm Sun-Thu, to 10pm Fri & Sat; ☑) Inside a converted brick-walled warehouse, Forchetta Bastoni has two kitchens that make wildly different food – Southeast Asian and Italian. Pick a cuisine, then be seated on one side or the other for wood-fired pizzas, pastas and roasted meats; or noodles, rice bowls and curries. If you can't decide, sit at the happening bar.

Red's Apple Roadhouse
American $$

(☑707-861-9338; www.redsappleroadhouse.com; 4550 Gravenstein Hwy N; mains $9-15; ⊙8am-9:30pm Tue-Sat, to 5pm Sun) ☑ A rustic road-house and tavern north of downtown (next door to Mom's Apple Pie), Red's smokes its own bacon and pastrami, bakes its own bread and serves simple, quality American cooking, using locally sourced ingredients in dishes like fried chicken and waffles, pulled-pork sandwiches, biscuits and gravy, and classic mac-n-cheese. Local beer and wine. Live music Wednesday and Friday evenings.

K&L Bistro
French $$$

(☑707-823-6614; www.klbistro.com; 119 S Main St; lunch $14-20, dinner $19-29; ⊙11am-9pm) K&L serves earthy provincial Cal-French bistro cooking in a convivial bar-and-grill space with sidewalk patio. Expect classics like mussels and French fries, and grilled steaks with red-wine reduction. Reservations essential.

Zazu Kitchen & Farm
Italian, New American $$$

(☑707-523-4814; zazukitchen.com; 6770 McKinley St, 150, The Barlow; lunch mains $13-18, dinner $24-29; ⊙11:30am-10pm Wed & Thu, to midnight Fri, from 9am Sat & Sun, from 5pm Mon) ☑ We love the farm-to-table ethos of Zazu – they raise their own pigs and source everything locally – but some dishes miss the mark, and the industrial-style space gets crazy loud. Still, we love their pizzas, salads, housemade salumi and bacon. Good breakfasts, too.

🍸 Drinking & Entertainment

Woodfour Brewing Co.
Brewery

(☑707-823-3144; www.woodfourbrewing.com; 6780 Depot St, The Barlow; ⊙11am-9pm Sun-Thu, to 11pm Fri & Sat) ☑ Woodfour's solar-powered brewery serves 12 housemade beers, light on alcohol and hops, plus several sours (high-acid beer). It has an exceptionally good menu of small plates, designed to pair with beer, from simple snacks to refined, technique-driven dishes better than any we've had at a California brewery.

Taylor Maid Farms
Cafe

(☑707-634-7129; www.taylormaidfarms.com; 6790 Depot St, The Barlow; ⊙6am-7pm Sun-Thu, to 9pm Fri & Sat) ☑ Choose your brew method (drip, press, etc) at this third-wave coffeehouse that roasts its own organic beans. Exceptional seasonal drinks include lavender lattes.

Jasper O'Farrell's
Bar

(☑707-823-1389; 6957 Sebastopol Ave; ⊙noon-2am) Busy bar with billiards and live music most nights; good drink specials.

Hopmonk Tavern
Live Music

(☑707-829-7300; www.hopmonk.com; 230 Petaluma Ave; ⊙11:30am-11pm Sun-Wed, to midnight Thu-Sat) This always-busy tavern and beer garden has the town's most diverse live-music calendar, and sometimes hosts the likes of Jonathan Richman.

🛍 Shopping

Antique shops line Gravenstein Hwy S toward Hwy 101.

Aubergine
Vintage

(☑707-827-3460; 755 Petaluma Ave; ⊙10am-6pm) Vast vintage emporium, specializing in cast-off European thrift-shop clothing.

Funk & Flash
Clothing

(☑707-829-1142; www.funkandflash.com; 228 S Main St; ⊙11am-7pm) Disco-glam party clothes, inspired by Burning Man.

Antique Society
Antiques

(☑707-829-1733; www.antiquesociety.com; 2661 Gravenstein Hwy S; ⊙10am-5pm) Boasts 125 antiques vendors under one roof.

Midgley's Country Flea Market
Market

(☑707-823-7874; mfleamarket.com; 2200 Gravenstein Hwy S; ⊙6:30am-4:30pm Sat & Sun) The region's largest flea market.

ℹ Information

Sebastopol Area Chamber of Commerce & Visitors Center (☑877-828-4748, 707-823-3032; www.visitsebastopol.org; 265 S Main St; ⊙10am-4pm Mon-Fri) Maps, information and exhibits.

Occidental & Around

At Christmastime, Bay Area families flock to Occidental to buy trees. The town decorates to the nines, and there's weekend cookie-decorating and caroling at the Union Hotel's Bocce Ballroom.

👁 Sights & Activities

Sonoma Canopy Tours — Outdoors

(☎ 888-494-7868; www.sonomacanopytours.com; 6250 Bohemian Hwy; adult $99-109, child $69) North of town, fly through the redwood canopy on seven interconnected ziplines, ending with an 80ft-rappel descent; reservations required.

Osmosis — Spa

(☎ 707-823-8231; www.osmosis.com; 209 Bohemian Hwy, Freestone; ⊙ by appointment) Three miles south in Freestone, tranquility prevails at this Japanese-inspired spa, which indulges patrons with dry-enzyme baths of aromatic cedar fibers (bath-and-blanket wrap $89 to $99), lovely tea-and-meditation gardens, plus outdoor massages. Make reservations.

🛏 Sleeping

Occidental Hotel — Motel $$

(☎ 877-867-6084, 707-874-3623; www.occidentalhotel. com; 3610 Bohemian Hwy; r $120-160, 2-bedroom q

---

A WINE COUNTRY PRIMER

When people talk about Sonoma, they're referring to the *whole* county which, unlike Napa, is huge. It extends all the way from the coast, up the Russian River Valley, into Sonoma Valley and eastward to Napa Valley; in the south it stretches from San Pablo Bay (an extension of San Francisco Bay) to Healdsburg in the north. It's essential to break Sonoma down by district.

West County refers to everything west of Hwy 101 and includes the Russian River Valley and the coast. Sonoma Valley stretches north–south along Hwy 12. In northern Sonoma County, Alexander Valley lies east of Healdsburg, and Dry Creek Valley lies north of Healdsburg. In the south, Carneros straddles the Sonoma–Napa border, north of San Pablo Bay. Each region has its own particular wines; what grows where depends upon the weather.

Inland valleys get hot; coastal regions stay cool. In West County and Carneros, night-time fog blankets the vineyards. Burgundy-style wines do best, particularly Pinot Noir and Chardonnay. Further inland, Alexander, Sonoma and much of Dry Creek Valley (as well as Napa Valley) are fog-protected. Here, Bordeaux-style wines thrive, especially Cabernet Sauvignon, Sauvignon Blanc, Merlot and other heat-loving varieties. For California's famous Cabernets, head to Napa. Zinfandel and Rhône-style varieties, such as Syrah and Viognier, grow in both regions, warm and cool. In cooler climes, wines are lighter and more elegant; in warmer areas they are heavier and more rustic. As you explore, notice the bases of grapevines: the fatter they are, the older. 'Old vine' grapes yield color and complexity not found in grapes from younger vines.

Some basics: wineries and vineyards aren't the same. Grapes grow in a vineyard, then get fermented at a winery. Wineries that grow their own grapes are called estates, as in 'estate-grown' or 'estate-bottled'; but estates, too, ferment grapes from other vineyards. When vintners speak of 'single-vineyard' or 'vineyard-designate' wines, they mean the grapes all originated from the same vineyard; this allows for tighter quality-control. 'Single varietal' means all the grapes are the same variety (such as 100% Merlot), but may come from different vineyards. Reserves are the vintner's limited-production wines; they're usually available only at the winery.

Don't be afraid to ask questions. Vintners love to talk. If you don't know how to taste wine, or what to look for, ask the person behind the counter to help you discover what you like. Just remember to spit out the wine; the slightest buzz will diminish your capacity to taste.

For a handy-dandy reference on the road, pick up a copy of Karen MacNeil's *The Wine Bible* (2001, Workman Publishing) or Jancis Robinson's *The Oxford Companion to Wine* (2006, Oxford University Press) to carry in the car.

Wild Flour Bread

$200-240; ❄ 🔊 ☕ 🐾) Rates are sometimes negotiable for these well-kept motel rooms.

Valley Ford Hotel
Inn $$
(☎ 707-876-1983; www.vfordhotel.com; r $115-175) Surrounded by pastureland 8 miles south in Valley Ford, this 19th-century, six-room inn has good beds, great rates and a terrific roadhouse restaurant.

Inn at Occidental
Inn $$$
(☎ 707-874-1047, 800-522-6324; www. innatoccidental.com; 3657 Church St; r incl breakfast $249-339; 🐾) One of Sonoma's finest, this beautifully restored 18-room Victorian inn is filled with collectible antiques; rooms have gas fireplaces and cozy feather beds.

✕ Eating

Howard Station Cafe
American $
(☎ 707-874-2838; www.howardstationcafe.com; 3811 Bohemian Hwy; mains $6-12; ⏱ 7am-2:30pm Mon-Fri, to 3pm Sat & Sun; ♿ 🐾) Big plates of comfort cooking and fresh-squeezed juices. Cash only.

Wild Flour Bread
Bakery $
(www.wildflourbread.com; 140 Bohemian Hwy, Freestone; items from $3; ⏱ 8:30am-6:30pm Fri-

Mon) Organic brick-oven sourdough breads, giant sticky buns and good coffee.

Bohemian Market
Deli $
(☎ 707-874-3312; 3633 Main St; ⏱ 8am-9pm) Occidental's best grocery store has an OK deli.

Rocker Oysterfeller's
New American $$
(☎ 707-876-1983; www.rockeroysterfellers.com; 14415 Hwy 1, Valley Ford; mains $13-24; ⏱ 5pm-8:30pm Thu & Fri, from 3pm Sat, from 10am Sun) We love the flavor-rich cooking at this Valley Ford roadhouse, which features barbecued oysters, local crab cakes, steaks and fried chicken. Great wine bar, too. On Sundays there's brunch.

Barley & Hops
Pub Food $$
(☎ 707-874-9037; www.barleynhops.com; 3688 Bohemian Hwy; mains $10-15; ⏱ 4-9:30pm Mon-Thu, from 11am Fri-Sun) Serves over 100 beers, sandwiches, giant salads and shepherd's pie.

Bistro des Copains
French-Californian $$$
(☎ 707-874-2436; www.bistrodescopains.com; 3728 Bohemian Hwy; mains $24-26, 3-course menu $40-45; ⏱ 5-9pm Wed-Mon) ✐ Worth a special trip, this convivial bistro draws bon vivants for Cal-French country cooking, like *steak-frites*

and roast duck. Great wines; $10 corkage for Sonoma vintages. Make reservations.

🛍 Shopping

Verdigris Homewares

(☑707-874-9018; www.1lightartlamps.com; 72 Main St; ⏰11am-6pm Thu-Mon) Crafts gorgeous art lamps.

Hand Goods Ceramics

(☑707-874-2161; www.handgoods.net; 3627 Main St; ⏰10am-6pm) Collective of ceramicists and potters.

Guerneville & Around

The Russian River's biggest vacation-resort town, Guerneville gets busy summer weekends with party-hardy gay boys, sun-worshipping lesbians and long-haired, beer-drinking Harley riders, earning it the nickname 'Groin-ville.' Though the town is slowly gentrifying, it hasn't lost its honky-tonk vibe – fun-seeking crowds still come to canoe, hike redwoods and hammer cocktails poolside.

Downriver, some areas are sketchy (due to drugs). The local chamber of commerce has chased most of the tweakers from Main St in Guerneville, but if some off-the-beaten-path areas feel creepy – especially campgrounds – they probably are.

Four miles downriver, tiny Monte Rio has a sign over Hwy 116 declaring it 'Vacation Wonderland' – an overstatement, but the dog-friendly beach is a hit with families. Further west, idyllic Duncans Mills is home to a few dozen souls and has picture-ready historic buildings, now converted into cute shops. Upriver, east of Guerneville, Forestville is where agricultural country resumes.

⊙ Sights & Activities

Look for sandy beaches and swimming holes along the river; there's good river access east of town at Sunset Beach (www.sonoma-county.org/parks; 11060 River Rd, Forestville; per car $7; ⏰7am-sunset). Fishing and watercraft outfitters operate mid-May to early October, after which winter rains dangerously swell the river. A farmers market meets downtown on Wednesdays, June through September, from 3pm to 7pm. On summer Saturdays, there's also one at Monte Rio Beach, 11am to 2pm.

Armstrong Redwoods State Natural Reserve Forest

See page 46

Burke's Canoe Trips Canoeing

(☑707-887-1222; www.burkescanoetrips.com; 8600 River Rd, Forestville; canoe/kayak rental incl shuttle $65/45; ⏰10am-6pm Mon-Fri, 9am-6pm Sat & Sun) You can't beat Burke's for a day on the river. Self-guided canoe and kayak trips include a shuttle back to your car. Make reservations; plan for four hours. Camping in its riverside redwood grove costs $10 per person.

R3 Hotel Pool Swimming

(Triple R; ☑707-869-8399; www.ther3hotel.com; 16390 4th St, Guerneville; ⏰9am-midnight) **FREE** The gay, adults-only, party-scene swimming pool at the Triple R is free, provided you buy drinks. Bring your own towel. Bathing suits mandatory, but only because state liquor-license laws require them.

Pee Wee Golf & Arcade Golf, Cycling

(☑707-869-9321; 16155 Drake Rd at Hwy 116, Guerneville; 18/36 holes $8/12; ⏰11am-10pm Jun-Aug, to 5pm Sat & Sun May & Sep; 🚻) Flashback to 1948 at this impeccably kept, retro-kitsch, 36-hole miniature golf course, just south of the Hwy 116 bridge, with brilliantly painted obstacles, including T Rex and Yogi Bear. Bring your own cocktails; also rents gas barbecue grills ($20).

King's Sport & Tackle Fishing, Kayaking, Canoeing

(☑707-869-2156; www.kingsrussianriver.com; 16258 Main St, Guerneville; ⏰8am-6pm) *The* local source for fishing and river-condition information. Also rents kayaks ($35 to $55), canoes ($55) and fishing gear.

River Rider Bicycle Rental

(☑707-483-2897; www.riverridersrentals.com; half-/full-day rental $25/45; ⏰7am-7pm) Delivers bicycles, along with wine-tasting passes on request; discounts for multiday rentals.

Johnson's Beach Water Sports

See page 47

Northwood Golf Course Golf

(☑707-865-1116; www.northwoodgolf.com; 19400 Hwy 116, Monte Rio; walking $25-27, riding $33-35, 9 holes $25-35, 18 holes $35-53; ⏰7:30am-sunset) Vintage-1920s Alistair MacKenzie–designed, par-36, nine-hole course.

⚜ Festivals & Events

Monte Rio Variety Show — Music

(www.monterioshow.org) Members of the elite, secretive Bohemian Grove (Google it) perform publicly, sometimes showcasing unannounced celebrities, in July.

Lazy Bear Weekend — Cultural

(www.lazybearweekend.com) Read: heavy, furry gay men; August. See p48 for more information.

Russian River Jazz & Blues Festival — Music

(www.russianriverfestivals.com) A day of jazz, followed by a day of blues in September, with occasional luminaries like BB King.

🛏 Sleeping

Russian River has few budget sleeps; prices drop midweek. For weekends and holidays, book ahead. Many places have no TVs. Because the river sometimes floods, some lodgings have cold linoleum floors: pack slippers.

Guerneville

Staying downtown means you can walk to restaurants and bars.

Guerneville Lodge — Campground $

(🖉 707-869-0102; www.guernevillelodge.com; 15905 River Rd; tent sites $40) The prettiest place to camp in downtown Guerneville is behind this retreat-center lodge, on sprawling grassy lawns fronting on the river. Amenities: hot clean showers, big campsites, refrigerator access, fire pits with grills. When available, lodge rooms cost $189 to $229.

Bullfrog Pond Campground — Campground $

(🖉 Mon-Fri reservations & information 707-869-9177, Sat & Sun ranger kiosk 707-869-2015; www.stewardscr.org; sites reserved/non-reserved $35/25; 🐾) Reached via a steep road from Armstrong Redwoods State Natural Reserve, 4 miles from the entrance kiosk, Bullfrog Pond has forested campsites, with cold water, and primitive hike-in and equestrian backcountry campsites. Reserve via www.hipcamp.com or by phone.

Fern Grove Cottages — Cabin $$

(🖉 707-869-8105; www.ferngrove.com; 16650 River Rd; cabins incl breakfast $159-219, with kitchen $199-269; @ 🖥 🏊 🐾) Downtown Guerneville's cheeriest resort, Fern Grove has vintage-1930s pine-paneled cabins, tucked beneath redwoods and surrounded by lush flowering gardens. Some have Jacuzzis and fireplaces. The pool is treated with salt, not chlorine; the lovely English innkeeper provides concierge services; and breakfast includes homemade scones.

Highlands Resort — Cabin, Campground $$

(🖉 707-869-0333; www.highlandsresort.com; 14000 Woodland Dr; tent sites $20-30, r with bath $90-100, without $70-80, cabins $120-205; 🖥 🏊 🐾) Guerneville's mellowest all-gay resort sits on a wooded hillside, walkable to town, and has simply furnished rooms, little cottages with porches and good camping. The large pool and hot tub are clothing-optional (weekday/weekend day use $10/15).

Applewood Inn — Inn $$$

(🖉 800-555-8509, 707-869-9093; www.applewoodinn.com; 13555 Hwy 116; r incl breakfast $215-345; ❄ @ 🏊) A hideaway estate on a wooded hilltop south of town, cushy Applewood has marvelous 1920s-era detail, with dark wood and heavy furniture that echo the forest. Rooms have Jacuzzis, couples' showers and top-end linens; some have fireplaces. Small on-site spa.

Boon Hotel + Spa — Boutique Hotel $$$

(🖉 707-869-2721; www.boonhotels.com; 14711 Armstrong Woods Rd; r $165-275; 🖥 🏊 🐾) 🚲 Rooms surround a swimming-pool courtyard (with Jacuzzi) at this mid-century-modern, 14-room motel-resort, gussied up in minimalist style. The look is austere but fresh, with organic-cotton linens and spacious rooms; most have wood-burning fireplaces. Drive to town, or ride the free bicycles.

Forestville

Raford Inn
B&B **$$$**

(📞 800-887-9503, 707-887-9573; http://rafordinn.com; 10630 Wohler Rd, Healdsburg; r $185-270; ❄️@🛜) 🍃 We love this 1880 Victorian B&B's secluded hilltop location, surrounded by tall palms and rambling vineyards. Rooms are big and airy, done with lace and antiques; some have fireplaces. And wow, those sunset views.

Farmhouse Inn
Inn **$$$**

(📞 800-464-6642, 707-887-3300; www.farmhouseinn.com; 7871 River Rd; r $445-795; ❄️@🛜🏊) Think love nest. The area's premier inn has spacious rooms and cottages, styled with cushy amenities like saunas, steam-showers and wood-burning fireplaces. Small on-site spa and top-notch restaurant. Check in early to maximize time.

Monte Rio
Village Inn
Inn **$$**

(📞 707-865-2304; www.villageinn-ca.com; 20822 River Blvd; r $145-235; 🛜) 🍃 A retired concierge owns this cute, old-fashioned, 11-room inn, beneath towering trees, right on the river. Some rooms have river views; all have fridge and microwave. No elevator.

Rio Villa Beach Resort
Inn **$$**

(📞 877-746-8455, 707-865-1143; www.riovilla.com; 20292 Hwy 116; r with kitchen $149-209, without $139-189; ❄️🛜🏊) Landscaping is lush at this small riverside resort with excellent sun exposure (you see redwoods, but you're not under them). Rooms are well kept but simple (request a quiet room, not by the road); the emphasis is on the outdoors, evident by the large riverside terrace, outdoor fireplace and barbecues. Some air-con.

Duncans Mills
Casini Ranch
Campground **$**

(📞 800-451-8400, 707-865-2255; www.casiniranch.com; 22855 Moscow Rd; tent sites $45-52, RV sites partial hookups $47-58, full hookups $53-56; 🛜🏊) In quiet Duncans Mills, beautifully set on riverfront ranchlands, Casini is an enormous, well-run campground. Amenities include kayaks and paddleboats (day use $5 to $10); bathrooms are spotless.

🍴 Eating

Guerneville

There's a good taco truck in the Safeway parking lot at 16451 Main St.

Big Bottom Market
Market, Cafe **$**

(📞 707-604-7295; www.bigbottommarket.com; 16228 Main St; sandwiches $7-10; ⏰8am-5pm Sun-Thu, to 6pm Fri & Sat) 🍃 Gourmet deli and wine shop with scrumptious pastries and grab-and-go picnic supplies.

Armstrong Redwoods State Natural Reserve (p46)

Coffee Bazaar
Cafe $

(📞707-869-9706; www.mycoffeeb.com; 14045 Armstrong Woods Rd; dishes $5-9; ⏰6am-8pm; 🛜) Happening cafe with salads, sandwiches and all-day breakfasts; adjoins a good used bookstore.

Seaside Metal Oyster Bar
Seafood $$

(📞707-604-7250; seasidemetal.com; 16222 Main St; dishes $11-16; ⏰5-10pm Wed-Sun) Unexpectedly urban for Guerneville, this storefront raw bar is an offshoot of San Francisco's Bar Crudo – one of the city's best – and showcases oysters, clams, lobster and exquisitely prepared raw-fish dishes. There's limited hot food, but it's overwrought: stick to raw.

Dick Blomster's Korean Diner
Korean, American $$

(📞707-896-8006; 16236 Main St; mains $15-20; ⏰5-10pm Sun-Thu, to 2am Fri & Sat Jun-Aug, to 11pm Fri & Sat Sep-May) By day a vintage-1940s coffee shop, by night a Korean-American diner with full bar, Dick Blomster's serves playfully tongue-in-cheek dishes, including fried PB&J sandwiches and 'the other KFC – Korean fried crack' – fried chicken with sugary-sweet brown sauce, which sure hits the spot after a night's drinking.

Boon Eat + Drink
Californian $$$

(📞707-869-0780; http://eatatboon.com; 16248 Main St; lunch mains $14-18, dinner $15-26; ⏰11am-3pm Mon,Tue, Thu & Fri, 5-9pm Mon-Fri, 10am-3pm & 5-10pm Sat & Sun) Locally sourced ingredients inform the seasonal, Cali-smart cooking at this tiny, always-packed, New American bistro, with cheek-by-jowl tables that fill every night. Make reservations or expect to wait.

Forestville

Canneti Roadhouse
Italian $$

(📞707-887-2232; http://cannetirestaurant.com; 6675 Front St; lunch mains $12-24, dinner $15-28; ⏰11:30am-3pm Wed-Sat, to 5pm Sun, 5:30-9pm Tue-Sun) 🍴 A Tuscan-born chef makes bona fide *cucina Italiana*, using quality ingredients from local farms, at this austere restaurant in downtown Forestville, worth the 15-minute drive from Guerneville. The menu ranges from simple brick-oven pizzas to an all-Tuscan, five-course tasting menu ($55, dinner only). When it's warm, sit on the patio beneath a giant redwood. Make reservations.

Farmhouse Inn
New American $$$

(📞707-887-3300; www.farmhouseinn.com; 7871 River Rd; 3-/4-course dinner $69/84; ⏰from 5.30pm Thu-Mon) 🍴 Special-occasion-worthy, Michelin-starred Farmhouse changes its seasonal Euro-Cal menu daily using locally raised, organic ingredients like Sonoma lamb, wild salmon and rabbit – the latter is the house specialty. Details are impeccable, from aperitifs in the garden to tableside cheese service; detractors call it precious. Make reservations.

Monte Rio

Don's Dogs
Fast Food $

(📞707-865-4190; cnr Bohemian Hwy & Hwy 116; sandwiches $4-12; ⏰9am-4pm Thu-Mon Oct-May, to 7pm daily Jun-Sep; 🛜) Gourmet hot dogs, wine, beer, simple breakfasts and coffee, behind the Rio Theater.

Highland Dell
German $$$

(📞707-865-2300; http://highlanddell.com; 21050 River Blvd; mains $20-22; ⏰4-10pm Fri-Tue Apr-Nov) A dramatic, three-story-high, chalet-style dining room with a river-view deck, Highland Dell makes pretty good German-inspired cooking, including steaks and schnitzel. Full bar.

Duncans Mills

Cape Fear Cafe
American $$

(📞707-865-9246; 25191 Main St; lunch mains $9-15, dinner $15-25; ⏰10am-8pm Mon & Thu, to 3pm Tue & Wed, to 9pm Fri-Sun) A country-Americana diner in a 19th-century grange, Cape Fear is visually charming, but it's erratic – except at weekend brunch, when the kitchen makes excellent Benedicts. Good stopover en route to the coast.

🍷 Drinking & Nightlife

Stumptown Brewery
Brewery

(www.stumptown.com; 15045 River Rd, Guerneville; ⏰11am-midnight Sun-Thu, to 2am Fri & Sat) Guerneville's best straight bar, 1 mile east of downtown, is gay-friendly and has a foot-stompin' jukebox, billiards, riverside beer garden, and several homemade brews. Pretty-good pub grub includes house-smoked barbecue.

Rainbow Cattle Company
Bar

(www.queersteer.com; 16220 Main St, Guerneville; ⏰noon-midnight Sun-Thu, to 2am Fri & Sat) The stalwart gay watering hole has pinball and shuffleboard.

Sophie's Cellars
Wine Bar

(📞707-865-1122; www.sophiescellars.com; 25179 Main St/Hwy 116, Duncans Mills; glasses $7-15; ⏰11am-5pm Mon, Thu, Sat & Sun, to 7pm Fri) The perfect stopover between river and coast, Sophie's rural wine bar pours glasses and tastes of local wine, and carries cheese, salami and a well-curated selection of bottles. Friday's 'locals happy hour' (4pm to 7pm) brings hors d'oeuvres, drink specials and a big crowd.

☆ Entertainment

Rio Theater
Cinema

(📞707-865-0913; www.riotheater.com; cnr Bohemian Hwy & Hwy 116, Monte Rio; adult/child $8/5; 🚻) Dinner and a movie take on new meaning at this vintage-WWII Quonset hut converted to a cinema in 1950, with a concession stand serving gourmet hot dogs with a drink and chips for just $7. In 2014 they finally added heating, but still supply blankets. Only in Monte Rio. Shows nightly (and sometimes Sunday afternoons), but call ahead, especially off-season.

Main Street Station
Cabaret

(📞707-869-0501; www.mainststation.com; 16280 Main St, Guerneville; ⏰7-10pm or 11pm; 🚻) FREE Hosts live acoustic-only jazz, blues and cabaret nightly in summer (weekends in winter), and families are welcome because the cabaret doubles as an American-Italian restaurant (stick to pizza).

Rio Nido Roadhouse
Live Music

(📞707-869-0821; www.rionidoroadhouse.com; 14540 Canyon Two, Rio Nido) Raucous roadhouse bar, off River Rd, 4 miles east of Guerneville, with an eclectic lineup of live bands. Shows start 6pm Saturday and sometimes Friday and Sunday, too; check website.

🛍 Shopping

Eight miles west of Guerneville, tiny Duncans Mills (pop 85) has good shopping in a handful of side-by-side businesses within weathered 19th-century cottages.

Mr Trombly's Tea & Table
Food & Drink

(www.mrtromblystea.com; 25185 Main St, Duncans Mills; ⏰10am-5pm Sun-Thu, to 6pm Sat & Sun) Different kinds of tea and teapots, plus quality kitchen gadgets and well-priced tableware.

Pig Alley
Jewelry

(📞707-865-2698; www.pigalleyshop.com; 25193 Main St, Duncans Mills; ⏰10:30am-5:30pm) Vast selection of handcrafted American-made jewelry: notable for gorgeous earrings.

ℹ Information

Russian River Chamber of Commerce & Visitors Center (📞707-869-9000, 877-644-9001; www.russianriver.com; 16209 1st St, Guerneville; ⏰10am-4:45pm Mon-Sat, plus 10am-3pm Sun May-Sep) For information and lodging referrals.

Russian River Visitors Center (📞707-869-4096; ⏰10am-3pm Oct-Apr, to 4pm May-Sep) At Korbel Winery (p47).

Healdsburg & Around

◉ Sights

Healdsburg Plaza
Square

See page 48

Healdsburg Museum
Museum

(📞707-431-3325; www.healdsburgmuseum.org; 221 Matheson St, Healdsburg; donation requested; ⏰11am-4pm Wed-Sun) Exhibits include compelling installations on northern Sonoma County history, with an emphasis on Healdsburg. Pick up the walking-tour pamphlet.

Healdsburg Public Library
Library

(📞707-433-3772; sonomalibrary.org; cnr Piper & Center Sts; ⏰10am-6pm Tue, Thu & Fri, to 8pm Wed, to 4pm Sat) Wine Country's leading oenology-reference library.

Healdsburg Veterans Memorial Beach
Beach

See page 48

Locals Tasting Room
Tasting Room

(📞707-857-4900; www.tastelocalwines.com; Geyserville Ave & Hwy 128, Geyserville; ⏰11am-6pm) FREE Eight miles north of Healdsburg, tiny Geyserville is home to this indie tasting room, which represents 12 small-production wineries with free tastings.

Farmers Markets
Market

(www.healdsburgfarmersmarket.org; Healdsburg) Discover Healdsburg's agricultural abundance at the Tuesday market (cnr Vine & North Sts; ⏰3:30pm-6pm Wed Jun-Oct) and Saturday market (⏰9am-noon Sat May-Nov), the latter held one block west of the plaza.

Farmers Market, Healdsburg
JUDY BELLAH/GETTY IMAGES ©

passes include towel and lawn seating, not chairs; summer weekends sell out immediately – arrive before 10:45am.

Russian River Adventures
Canoeing

(☑ 707-433-5599; russianriveradventures.com; 20 Healdsburg Ave, Healdsburg; adult/child $50/25; 🚣 🐾) Paddle a secluded stretch of river in quiet inflatable canoes, stopping for rope swings, swimming holes, beaches and bird-watching. This ecotourism outfit points you in the right direction and shuttles you back at day's end. Or they'll guide your kids downriver while you go wine-tasting (guides $125 per day). Reservations required.

Getaway Adventures
Cycling, Kayaking

(☑ 800-499-2453, 707-763-3040; www.getaway-adventures.com) Guides spectacular morning vineyard cycling in Dry Creek Valley, followed by lunch and optional kayaking on Russian River ($150 to $175).

River's Edge Kayak & Canoe Trips
Boating

(☑ 707-433-7247; www.riversedgekayakandcanoe.com; 13840 Healdsburg Ave, Healdsburg) Rents hard-sided canoes ($90/110 per half/full day) and kayaks ($40/55). Self-guided rentals include shuttle.

🍃 Courses

The Shed
Course

Healdsburg's culinary center (p113) leads classes and workshop on topics related to food and sustainability, from seed-saving and bee-keeping, to home-brewing and kombucha-fermenting. Also hosts important lecturers, such as Michael Pollan.

Relish Culinary Adventures
Cooking Course

(☑ 707-431-9999, 877-759-1004; www.relishculinary.com; 14 Matheson St, Healdsburg; ⊙ by appointment) Plug into the locavore food scene with culinary day trips, demo-kitchen classes or winemaker dinners.

🎡 Festivals & Events

Russian River Wine Road Barrel Tasting
Wine

(www.wineroad.com) Sample wine directly from the cask, before it's bottled or released for sale, in March.

Future Farmers Parade
Cultural

(www.healdsburgfair.org) The whole town shows up for this classic-Americana farm parade in May.

🏃 Activities

After you've walked around the plaza, there isn't much to do in town. Go wine-tasting in Dry Creek Valley or Russian River Valley (p100). Bicycling on winding West Dry Creek Rd is brilliant, as is paddling the Russian River, which runs through town. Rent bikes from Spoke Folk Cyclery (☑ 707-433-7171; www.spokefolk.com; 201 Center St; ⊙ 10am-6pm Mon-Fri, to 5pm Sat & Sun).

Coppola Winery Swimming Pool
Swimming, Winery

(☑ 707-857-1400, 877-590-3329; www.francisfordcoppolawinery.com; 300 Via Archimedes, Geyserville; adult/child $30/15; ⊙ 11am-6pm daily Jun-Sep, Fri-Sun Apr, May & Oct; 🚣) The two huge interconnected pools at Francis Ford Coppola Winery are a glam way to spend a hot day with kids. To ensure admission, reserve in advance a cabine ($135), which includes chairs for four and wine-tasting passes; day

Wine & Food Affair   Food

(www.wineroad.com/events) Special food and wine pairings at over 100 wineries in November.

🛏 Sleeping

Healdsburg is expensive: demand exceeds supply. Rates drop winter to spring, but not significantly. Guerneville is much less expensive, and just 20 minutes away. Most Healdsburg inns are within walking distance of the plaza; several B&Bs are in the surrounding countryside. Find motels at Hwy 101's Dry Creek exit.

Cloverdale Wine Country KOA   Campground $

(☑800-368-4558, 707-894-3337; www.winecountry koa.com; 1166 Asti Ridge Rd, Cloverdale; tent/RV sites from $50/65, 1-/2-bedroom cabins $85/95; 🛜❄💺) Six miles from central Cloverdale (exit 520) off Hwy 101; hot showers, pool, hot tub, laundry, paddleboats and bicycles.

L&M Motel   Motel $$

(☑707-433-6528; www.landmmotel.com; 70 Healdsburg Ave, Healdsburg; r $150-180; ❄🛜💺🐾) Simple, clean, old-fashioned motel, with big lawns and barbecue grills, great for families. Dry sauna and Jacuzzi. Winter rates plummet.

Geyserville Inn   Motel $$

(☑877-857-4343, 707-857-4343; www.geyservilleinn. com; 21714 Geyserville Ave, Geyserville; r Mon-Fri $129-169, Sat & Sun $269-289; ❄🛜💺🐾) Eight miles north of Healdsburg, this immaculately kept upmarket motel is surrounded by vineyards. Rooms have unexpectedly smart furnishings and quality extras, like feather pillows. Request a remodeled room. Hot tub.

Hotel Healdsburg   Hotel $$$

(☑707-431-2800, 800-889-7188; www. hotelhealdsburg.com; 25 Matheson St, Healdsburg; r incl breakfast from $450; ❄@💺🐾) Smack on the plaza, the fashion-forward HH has a coolly minimalist style of concrete and velvet, with requisite top-end amenities, including sumptuous beds and extra-deep tubs. Full-service spa.

H2 Hotel   Hotel $$$

(☑707-431-2202, 707-922-5251; www.h2hotel.com; 219 Healdsburg Ave, Healdsburg; r incl breakfast Mon-Fri $289-389, Sat & Sun $409-509; ❄@🛜💺) 🌿 Little sister to Hotel Healdsburg, H2 has the same angular concrete style, but was built LEED-gold-certified from the ground up, with a living roof, reclaimed everything, and fresh-looking rooms with cushy organic linens. Tiny pool, free bikes.

Madrona Manor   Historic Hotel $$$

(☑800-258-4003, 707-433-4231; www. madronamanor.com; 1001 Westside Rd, Healdsburg; r incl breakfast Mon-Fri $260-305, Sat & Sun $385-515; ❄🛜💺) The first choice of lovers of country inns and stately manor homes, the regal 1881 Madrona Manor exudes Victorian elegance. Surrounded by 8 acres of woods and gorgeous century-old gardens, the hilltop mansion is decked out with many original furnishings. A mile west of downtown, it's convenient to Westside Rd wineries.

Belle de Jour Inn   B&B $$$

(☑707-431-9777; www.belledejourinn.com; 16276 Healdsburg Ave, Healdsburg; r $225-295, ste $355; ❄🛜) Charming Belle de Jour's sunny, uncluttered rooms have American-country furnishings, with extras like private entrances, sun-dried sheets and jetted tubs. The manicured gardens are ready-made for a moonlight tryst.

🍴 Eating

Healdsburg is the gastronomic capital of Sonoma County. Your hardest decision will be choosing where to eat. Reservations essential.

★ The Shed   Cafe, Market $

(☑707-431-7433; healdsburgshed.com; 25 North St, Healdsburg; dishes $3-15; ⏰8am-7pm Wed-Mon; 🍴) 🌿 At the vanguard of locavore eating, the Shed integrates food at all stages of production, milling its own locally sourced flours, pressing olive oils, fermenting vinegars and kombucha from local fruit, and growing its own produce. It comprises a cafe with wood-fired dishes, fermentation bar with housemade shrubs, coffee bar with stellar pastries, and a market with prepared to-go foods.

Healdsburg Bar & Grill   Pub Food $$

(☑707-433-3333; www.healdsburgbarandgrill.com; 245 Healdsburg Ave, Healdsburg; mains $9-15; ⏰8am-9pm) 'Top Chef Masters' winner Doug Keane's gastropub is perfect when you're famished, but don't want to fuss. Expect simple classics – mac-n-cheese, pulled-pork sandwiches, top-end burgers and truffle-parmesan fries. At breakfast, look for homemade bagels and waffles. Sit in the garden.

Oakville Grocery
Deli $$

(☎707-433-3200; www.oakvillegrocery.com; 124 Matheson St, Healdsburg; sandwiches $10; ☺8am-7pm) Luxurious smoked fish and caviar, fancy sandwiches and grab-and-go gourmet picnics. It's overpriced, but the plaza-view fireside terrace is ever-fun for scouting Botox blonds, while nibbling cheese and sipping vino.

★ Madrona Manor
Californian $$$

(☎800-258-4003, 707-433-4231; www.madrona manor.com; 1001 Westside Rd, Healdsburg; 6-/11-course menu $106/$129; ☺6-9pm Wed-Sun) 🍴 You'd be hard-pressed to find a lovelier place to propose than this retro-formal Victorian mansion's garden-view verandah, though there's nothing old-fashioned about the artful haute cuisine: the kitchen churns its own butter, each course comes with a different variety of just-baked bread, lamb and cheese originate down the road, and desserts include ice cream flash-frozen tableside. Reserve a pre-sunset table on the verandah.

Mateo's Cucina Latina
Mexican $$$

(☎707-433-1520; www.mateoscocinalatina. com; 214 Healdsburg Ave, Healdsburg; small plates $11-15, mains $21-25; ☺11:30am-9pm Thu-Tue, 4-9pm Wed, closed Tue Nov-Apr) 🍴 This is not Mexican food as you may know it. Here the upmarket Yucatan-inspired cooking integrates fine technique and all-local ingredients for standout small plates, such as wild-nettle empanadas and slow-roasted suckling pig, whose subtle flavors shine through the spice. The full bar showcases rare tequilas and mescals. Make reservations; request a garden table.

Self-Catering
Dry Creek General Store
Deli $

(☎707-433-4171; www.drycreekgeneralstore1881. com; 3495 Dry Creek Rd, Healdsburg; sandwiches $8-10; ☺6:30am-6pm) Stop at this vintage general store, where locals and cyclists gather for coffee on the creaky front porch. Perfect picnic supplies include Toscano-salami-and-manchego sandwiches on ciabatta.

Cheese Shop
Food $

(☎707-433-4998; www.sharpandnutty.com; 423 Center St, Healdsburg; ☺11am-6pm Mon-Sat) Top-notch imported and local cheeses.

Noble Folk Ice Cream & Pie Bar
Desserts $

(☎707-395-4426; 116 Matheson St, Healdsburg; slice $5.25, single cone $3.25; ☺noon-9pm) 🍴 Hand-crafted ice cream and classic American pie, made with top-quality, all-local ingredients.

🍷 Drinking & Entertainment

Flying Goat Coffee
Cafe

(www.flyinggoatcoffee.com; 324 Center St, Healdsburg; ☺7am-7pm) 🍴 See ya later, Starbucks. Flying Goat is what coffee should be – fair-trade and house-roasted – and locals line up for it every morning.

Bear Republic Brewing Company
Brewery

(☎707-433-2337; www.bearrepublic.com; 345 Healdsburg Ave, Healdsburg; ☺11am-9:30pm Sun-Thu, to 11pm Fri & Sat) Bear Republic features handcrafted award-winning ales, non-award-winning pub grub, and live music weekends.

Alexander Valley Bar
Cocktail Bar

(AVB; ☎707-431-1904; 3487 Alexander Valley Rd, Medlock Ames Winery; ☺5-9pm Sun-Thu, to 11pm Fri & Sat) Vineyard sunsets are incredible at this speakeasy-style bar in Alexander Valley, which crafts cocktails ($10) using whatever's growing in the garden outside.

Raven Theater & Film Center
Theater

(☎707-433-5448; www.raventheater.com; 115 N Main St, Healdsburg) Hosts concerts, events and first-run art-house films.

🛍 Shopping

The Shed
Garden, Culinary

(☎707-431-7433; healdsburgshed.com; 25 North St, Healdsburg; ☺8am-7pm Wed-Mon) 'Tools and supplies for growing, preparing and sharing food,' including heritage seeds by local farmers, house-milled California flour, and practical cookware.

Levin & Company
Books, Music

(☎707-433-1118; 306 Center St, Healdsburg; ☺9am-9pm Mon-Sat, 10am-6pm Sun) Fiction and CDs; co-op art gallery.

❶ Information

Healdsburg Chamber of Commerce & Visitors Bureau (☎707-433-6935, 800-648-9922; www.healdsburg.com; 217 Healdsburg Ave; ☺9am-5pm Mon-Fri, to 3pm Sat, 10am-2pm Sun) A block south of the plaza. Has winery maps and information on ballooning, golf, tennis, spas and nearby farms (get the *Farm Trails* brochure); 24-hour walk-up booth.

Bodega Bay

Bodega Bay is the first pearl in a string of sleepy fishing towns that line the North Coast and was the setting of Hitchcock's terrifying 1963 avian psycho-horror flick *The Birds*. The skies are free from bloodthirsty gulls today (though you best keep an eye on the picnic); it's Bay Area weekenders who descend en masse for extraordinary beaches, tide pools, whale-watching, fishing, surfing and seafood. Mostly a few restaurants, hotels and shops on both sides of Hwy 1, the downtown is not made for strolling, but it is a great base for exploring the endless nearby coves of the Sonoma Coast State Beach (p117).

Originally inhabited by the Pomo people, the bay takes its name from Juan Francisco de la Bodega y Quadra, captain of the Spanish sloop *Sonora*, which entered the bay in 1775. The area was then settled by Russians in the early 19th century, and farms were established to grow wheat for the Russian fur-trapping empire, which stretched from Alaska all the way down the coast to Fort Ross. The Russians pulled out in 1842, abandoning fort and farms, and American settlers moved in.

Hwy 1 runs through town and along the east side of Bodega Bay. On the west side, a peninsula juts out to sea, forming the entrance to Bodega Harbor.

- - - - - - - - - - - - - - - - - -

◉ Sights & Activities

Surfing, beachcombing and sportfishing are the main activities here – the latter requires advance booking. From December to April, the fishing boats host whale-watching trips, which are also good to book ahead. Just about everyone in town sells kites which are great for flying at Bodega Head. The excellent *Farm Trails* (www.farmtrails.org) guide at the Sonoma Coast Visitor Center (p116) has suggestions for tours of local ranches, orchards, farms and apiaries.

Bodega Head   Lookout

At the peninsula's tip, Bodega Head rises 265ft above sea level. To get there (and see the open ocean), head west from Hwy 1 onto Eastshore Rd, then turn right at the stop sign onto Bay Flat Rd. It's great for whale-watching. Landlubbers enjoy hiking above the surf, where several good trails include a 3.75-mile trek to Bodega Dunes Campground and a 2.2-mile walk to Salmon Creek Ranch.

Bodega Marine Laboratory & Reserve   Science Center

(☑707-875-2211; www.bml.ucdavis.edu; 2099 Westside Rd; ⊙2-4pm Fri) FREE Run by University of California (UC) Davis, this spectacularly diverse teaching and research reserve surrounds the research lab, which has studied Bodega Bay since the 1920s. The 263-acre reserve hosts many marine environments, including rocky intertidal coastal areas, mudflats and sandflats, salt marsh, sand dunes and freshwater wetlands. On most Friday afternoons docents give tours of the lab and surrounds.

Ren Brown Collection Gallery   Gallery

(www.renbrown.com; 1781 Hwy 1; ⊙10am-5pm Wed-Sun) The renowned collection of modern Japanese prints and Californian works at this small gallery is a tranquil escape from the elements. Check out the Japanese garden at the back.

Chanslor Ranch   Horseback Riding

(☑707-785-8849; www.chanslorranch.com; 2660 N Hwy 1; rides from $40) Just north of town, this friendly outfit leads horseback expeditions along the coastline and the rolling inland hills. Ron, the trip leader, is an amiable, sun-weathered cowboy straight from central casting; he recommends taking the Salmon Creek ride or calling ahead for weather-permitting moonlight rides. The 90-minute beach rides are donation based, and support a horse-rescue program.

Overnight trips in simple platform tents, which are excellent for families, can also be arranged. If you book a ride, you can park your RV at the ranch for free.

Bodega Bay Sportfishing Center   Fishing, Whale-Watching

(☑707-875-3344; www.bodegacharters.com; 1410 Bay Flat Rd) Beside the Sandpiper Cafe, this outfit organizes full-day fishing trips ($135) and whale-watching excursions (three hours adult/child $50/35). It also sells bait, tackle and fishing licenses. Call ahead to ask about recent sightings.

Bodega Bay Surf Shack   Surfing

(☑707-875-3944; http://bodegabaysurf.com; 1400 N Hwy 1; surfboard/wetsuit/kayak rentals from $17/17/45) If you want to get on the water, this easygoing one-stop shop has all kinds of rentals, lessons and good local information.

⚜ Festivals & Events

Bodega Bay Fishermen's Festival Cultural
(www.bbfishfest.org) At the end of April, this
festival culminates in a blessing of the fleet,
a flamboyant parade of vessels, an arts-and-
crafts fair, kite-flying and feasting.

**Bodega Seafood, Art &
Wine Festival** Food, Wine
(www.winecountryfestivals.com; 🐾) In late August, this festival of food and drink brings
together the best beer- and wine-makers of
the area, tons of seafood and activities for
kids. It takes place in the town of Bodega.

🛏 Sleeping

There's a wide spread of options – RV and
tent camping, quaint motels and fancy hotels. All fill up early during peak seasons.
Campers should consider heading just north
of town to the state-operated sites.

**Sonoma County
Regional Parks** Campground $
(☎707-565-2267; www.parks.sonomacounty.ca.gov;
tent sties $7, RV sites without hookups $32) There
are a few walk-in sites at Doran Regional
Park's (201 Doran Beach Rd) quiet Miwok Tent
Campground, and Westside Regional Park
(2400 Westshore Rd), which is best for RVs. It
caters primarily to boaters and has windy
exposures, beaches, hot showers, fishing and
boat ramps. Both are heavily used. Excellent
camping is also available at the Sonoma
Coast State Beach (p117).

Bodega Harbor Inn Motel $$
(☎707-875-3594; www.bodegaharborinn.com; 1345
Bodega Ave; r $80-155, cottages $135-175; 🐾🐕)
Half a block inland from Hwy 1, surrounded
by grassy lawns and furnished with both
real and faux antiques, this modest yet ador-
able blue-and-white shingled motel is the
town's most economical option. Pets are al-
lowed in some rooms for a fee of $15 plus a
security deposit of $50. Also offers a variety
of cottages and rentals around town.

Bodega Bay Lodge & Spa Lodge $$$
(☎888-875-2250, 707-875-3525; www.bodegabay
lodge.com; 103 Hwy 1; r $190-470; @🐾🐕) Bo-
dega's plushest option, this small oceanfront
resort has an ocean-view swimming pool,
golf course, a Jacuzzi and a fitness club. In the
evenings it hosts wine tastings. The more expensive rooms have commanding views, but
all have balconies. The other pluses on-site
include Bodega Bay's best spa and the Duck
Club (☎707-875-3525; mains $16-37; ⊙7:30-11am &
6-9pm), which is the fanciest dining in town.

🍴 Eating & Drinking

For the old-fashioned thrill of seafood by the
docks there are two options: Tides Wharf
& Restaurant (835 Hwy 1; breakfast $8-22, lunch
$13-28, dinner $16-28; ⊙7:30am-9:30pm Mon-Thu,
7:30am-10pm Fri, 7am-10pm Sat, 7am-9:30pm Sun;
🐾) and Lucas Wharf Restaurant & Bar (595
Hwy 1; mains $9-28; ⊙11:30am-9pm Mon-Fri, 11am-
10pm Sat; 🐾). Both have views and similar
menus of clam chowder, fried fish and cole-
slaw, and markets for picnic supplies. Tides
boasts a great fish market, though Lucas
Wharf feels less like a factory. Don't be surprised if a bus pulls up outside either of them.

The Birds Cafe Mexican, American $
(1407 Hwy 1; meals $6-14; ⊙11:30am-5pm) The
menu consists of just a few things – usually
fish tacos, fish 'n' chips, chowder and a few
salads. Barbecued oysters are available sea-
sonally. Order at the bar then take it to an
outdoor picnic table overlooking the harbor. There's beer and wine available. Bliss.

**Terrapin Creek Cafe
& Restaurant** Californian $$
(☎707-875-2700; www.terrapincreekcafe.com; 1580
Eastshore Dr; lunch mains $12-19, dinner mains $23-
30; ⊙11am-2:30pm & 4:30-9pm Thu-Sun; 🐾) 🍃
Bodega Bay's most exciting upscale restau-
rant is run by a husband-wife team who
espouse the slow food movement and serve
local dishes sourced from the surrounding
area. Comfort-food offerings like black cod
roasted in lemon grass and coconut broth
are artfully executed, while the Dungeness
crab salad is fresh, briny and perfect. Jazz
and warm light complete the atmosphere.

Gourmet Au Bay Wine Bar
(913 Hwy 1; ⊙11am-6pm Thu-Tue) The back deck
of this wine bar offers a salty breeze with
wine tasting.

ℹ Information

Sonoma Coast Visitor Center (☎707-875-
3866; www.bodegabay.com; 850 Hwy 1; ⊙9am-
5pm Mon-Thu & Sat, to 6pm Fri, 10am-5pm Sun)
Opposite the Tides Wharf. Stop by for the best
help on the coast and for a copy of the *North
Coaster*, a small-press indie newspaper of es-
says and brilliant insights on local culture.

JASON TODD/GETTY IMAGES ©

Bodega Head (p115)

Sonoma Coast State Beach

Stretching 17 miles north from Bodega Head to Vista Trail, the glorious Sonoma Coast State Beach (☎707-875-3483) is actually a series of beaches separated by several beautiful rocky headlands. Some beaches are tiny, hidden in little coves, while others stretch far and wide. Most of the beaches are connected by vista-studded coastal hiking trails that wind along the bluffs. Exploring this area makes an excellent day-long adventure, so bring a picnic. Be advised however: the surf is often too treacherous to wade, so keep an eye on children. While this system of beaches and parks has some camping, you can't just pitch a tent anywhere; most are for day-use only.

◉ Sights & Activities

Salmon Creek Beach   Beach
Situated around a lagoon, this has 2 miles of hiking and good waves for surfing.

**Portuguese Beach &
Schoolhouse Beach**   Beaches
Both are very easy to access and have sheltered coves between rocky outcroppings.

Duncan's Landing   Beach
Small boats unload near this rocky headland in the morning. A good place to spot wildflowers in the spring.

Shell Beach   Beach
A boardwalk and trail leads out to a stretch perfect for tide-pooling and beachcombing.

Goat Rock   Beach
Famous for its colony of harbor seals, lazing in the sun at the mouth of the Russian River.

⊨ Sleeping

Bodega Dunes   Campground $
(☎800-444-7275; www.reserveamerica.com; 3095 Hwy 1, Bodega Bay; tent & RV sites $35, day use $8) The largest campground in the Sonoma Coast State Beach system of parks, it is also closest to Bodega Bay. It gets a lot of use. Sites are in high dunes and have hot showers but be warned – the fog horn sounds all night.

Wright's Beach Campground   Campground $
(☎800-444-7275; www.reserveamerica.com; tent & RV sites $35, day use $8) Of the few parks that allow camping along Sonoma Coast State Beach, this is the best, even though sites lack privacy. Sites can be booked six months in advance, and numbers 1–12 are right on the beach. There are BBQ pits for day use and it's a perfect launch for sea kayakers.

Everyone else, stay out of the water; according to camp hosts the treacherous rip tides claim a life every season.

Jenner

Perched on the hills looking out to the Pacific and above the mouth of the Russian River, tiny Jenner offers access to the coast and the Russian River wine region. A harbor-seal colony sits at the river's mouth and pups are born here from March to August. There are restrictions about getting too close to the chubby, adorable pups – handling them can be dangerous and cause the pups to be abandoned by their mothers. Volunteers answer questions along the roped-off area where day trippers can look on at a distance. The best way to see them is by kayak and most of the year you will find Water Treks Ecotours (☑707-865-2249; 2hr rental from $25; ⊙10am-3pm) renting kayaks on the highway. Heading north on Hwy 1 you will begin driving on one of the most beautiful, windy stretches of California highway. You'll also probably lose cell-phone service – possibly a blessing.

- -

🛏 Sleeping & Eating

Jenner Inn & Cottages   Inn $$

(☑707-865-2377; www.jennerinn.com; 10400 Hwy 1; r incl breakfast creekside $118-278, cottages $228-298; ⊚) It's difficult to sum up this collection of properties dispersed throughout Jenner – some are in fairly deluxe ocean-view cottages with kitchen and ready-to-light fireplaces, others are small and upland near a creek. All have the furnishings of a stylish auntie from the early 1990s.

★ Café Aquatica   Cafe $

(www.cafeaquatica.com; 10439 Hwy 1; sandwiches $10-13; 🖥) This is the kind of North Coast coffee shop you've been dreaming of: fresh pastries, organic coffee and chatty locals. The view of the Russian River from the patio and gypsy sea-hut decor make it hard to leave.

★ River's End   Californian $$$

(☑707-865-2484; www.rivers-end.com; 11048 Hwy 1; lunch mains $14-26, dinner mains $25-39; ⊙noon-3pm & 5-8:30pm Thu-Mon; 🖉) Unwind in style at this picture-perfect restaurant that overlooks the river's mouth and the grand sweep of the Pacific Ocean. It serves world-class meals at world-class prices, but the real reward is the view. Its ocean-view cottages (rooms and cottages $159 to $229) are wood paneled and have no TVs, wi-fi or phones. Not recommended for children under 12.

Sonoma coast

California Driving Guide

With jaw-dropping scenery and one of the USA's most comprehensive highway networks, California is an all-star destination for a road trip any time of year.

Driving Fast Facts

Right or left? Drive on the right

Legal driving age 16

Top speed limit 70mph (some interstate and state highways)

Best bumper sticker Mystery Spot, Santa Cruz

DRIVER'S LICENSE & DOCUMENTS

Out-of-state and international visitors may legally drive a car in California for up to 12 months with their home driver's license. If you're driving into the USA from Canada or Mexico, bring your vehicle's registration papers, liability insurance and home driver's license; an International Driving Permit (IDP) is a good supplement but isn't currently required.

If you're from overseas, an IDP will have more credibility with traffic police and will simplify the car-rental process, especially if your license doesn't have a photo or isn't written in English. International automobile associations can issue IDPs, valid for one year, for a fee. Always carry your home license together with the IDP.

The American Automobile Association (AAA) has reciprocal agreements with some international auto clubs (eg Canada's CAA, AA in the UK), so bring your membership card from home.

INSURANCE

California law requires liability insurance for all vehicles. When renting a car, check your home auto-insurance policy or your travel-insurance policy to see if rental cars are already covered. If not, expect to pay about $20 per day for liability insurance when renting a car.

Insurance against damage to the car itself, called Collision Damage Waiver (CDW) or Loss Damage Waiver (LDW), costs another $20 per day for rental cars. The deductible may require you to pay up to the first $500 for any repairs. If you decline CDW, you will be held liable for all damages up to the full value of the car.

Some credit cards cover CDW/LDW, provided you charge the entire cost of the car rental to that card. If you have an accident, you may have to pay the rental-car company first, then seek reimbursement. Most credit-card coverage isn't valid for rentals over 15 days or for 'exotic' models (eg convertibles, 4WD Jeeps).

RENTAL VEHICLES

To rent your own wheels, you'll typically need to be at least 25 years old, hold a valid driver's license and have a major credit card, *not* a check or debit card.

Road Distances (miles)

	Anaheim	Arcata	Bakersfield	Death Valley	Las Vegas	Los Angeles	Monterey	Napa	Palm Springs	Redding	Sacramento	San Diego	San Francisco	San Luis Obispo	Santa Barbara	Sth Lake Tahoe
Arcata	680															
Bakersfield	135	555														
Death Valley	285	705	235													
Las Vegas	265	840	285	140												
Los Angeles	25	650	110	290	270											
Monterey	370	395	250	495	535	345										
Napa	425	265	300	545	590	400	150									
Palm Springs	95	760	220	300	280	110	450	505								
Redding	570	140	440	565	725	545	315	190	650							
Sacramento	410	300	280	435	565	385	185	60	490	160						
San Diego	95	770	230	350	330	120	465	520	140	665	505					
San Francisco	405	280	285	530	570	380	120	50	490	215	85	500				
San Luis Obispo	225	505	120	365	405	200	145	265	310	430	290	320	230			
Santa Barbara	120	610	145	350	360	95	250	370	205	535	395	215	335	105		
Sth Lake Tahoe	505	400	375	345	460	480	285	160	485	260	100	600	185	390	495	
Yosemite	335	465	200	300	415	310	200	190	415	325	160	430	190	230	345	190

Rates generally include unlimited mileage, but expect surcharges for additional drivers and one-way rentals. Airport locations may have cheaper rates but higher fees; if you get a fly-drive package, local taxes may be extra when you pick up the car. Child or infant safety seats are compulsory; reserve them when booking your car.

Major car-rental companies:

Alamo (www.alamo.com)

Avis (www.avis.com)

Budget (www.budget.com)

Dollar (www.dollar.com)

Enterprise (www.enterprise.com)

Fox (www.foxrentacar.com)

Hertz (www.hertz.com)

National (www.nationalcar.com)

Thrifty (www.thrifty.com)

Some major car-rental companies offer 'green' fleets of hybrid or biofuel rental cars, but they're in short supply; make reservations far in advance and expect to pay significantly more for these models. Many companies rent hand-controlled vehicles and vans with wheelchair lifts at no extra charge, but you must also reserve these well in advance.

For independent car rentals, check:

Simply Hybrid (www.simplyhybrid.com) Hybrid car rentals in LA.

Zipcar (www.zipcar.com) Car-sharing club with two dozen California locations.

Car Rental Express (www.carrental express.com) Search for independent car-rental agencies.

Rent-a-Wreck (www.rentawreck.com) Rents to younger drivers, mainly in the LA and San Francisco Bay areas.

Super Cheap! Car Rental (www.super cheapcar.com) Rents to younger drivers in LA, Orange County and San Francisco Bay Area.

Wheelchair Getaways (www.wheelchair getaways.com) Rents wheelchair-accessible vans in San Francisco, LA and San Diego.

Motorcycles

Motorcycle rentals and insurance are very expensive. Discounts may be available for three-day and weekly rentals.

Eagle Rider (www.eaglerider.com) Nationwide compnay with 10 locations in California.

Dubbelju Motorcycle Rentals (www.dubbelju.com; 689a Bryant St, San Francisco)

Route 66 (www.route66riders.com) Harley Davidson rentals in LA's South Bay.

Recreational Vehicles & Campervans

Book Recreational Vehicle (RV) and campervan rentals as far in advance as possible. Rental costs vary by size and model; rates often don't include mileage, bedding or kitchen kits, vehicle prep or taxes. Pets are sometimes allowed (surcharge may apply).

Cruise America (www.cruiseamerica.com) Over 20 RV-rental locations statewide.

El Monte (www.elmonterv.com) Has 15 locations across California and offers AAA discounts.

Happy Travel Campers (www.camperusa.com) Rentals in San Francisco and LA.

Vintage Surfari Wagons (www.vwsurfari.com) LA-based rentals.

MAPS

Visitor centers and tourist information offices distribute free (but often very basic) maps. GPS navigation cannot be entirely relied upon, especially in remote desert or mountain areas. If you are planning on doing a lot of driving, you'll need a more detailed road map or atlas. Benchmark Maps' comprehensive *California Road & Recreation Atlas* ($25) is the gold standard, showing campgrounds, recreational areas and topographical land features, although it's less useful for navigating congested urban areas. Members of the American Automobile Association (AAA) or its international affiliates can pick up free driving maps from any of AAA's California offices.

ROAD HAZARDS & CONDITIONS

For highway conditions, including road closures and construction updates, dial ☎800-427-7623 or visit www.dot.ca.gov.

In places where winter driving is an issue, snow tires and tire chains may be required, especially on mountain highways. Ideally, carry your own chains and learn how to use them before you hit the road. Otherwise, chains can usually be bought (but not cheaply) on the highway, at gas stations or in nearby towns. Most car-rental companies don't permit the use of chains. Driving off-road, or on unpaved roads, is also prohibited by most car-rental companies.

In rural areas, livestock sometimes graze next to unfenced roads. These areas are typically signed as 'Open Range,' with the silhouette of a steer. Where deer or other wild animals frequently appear roadside, you'll see signs with the silhouette of a leaping deer. Take these signs seriously, particularly at night or in the fog.

In coastal areas, thick fog may impede driving – slow down and if it's too soupy, get off the road. Along coastal cliffs and on twisting mountain roads, watch out for falling rocks, mudslides and snow avalanches that could damage or disable your car if struck.

ROAD RULES

➡ Drive on the right-hand side of the road.

➡ Talking or texting on a cell (mobile) phone while driving is illegal.

➡ The use of seat belts is required for drivers, front-seat passengers and children under 16.

➡ Infant and child safety seats are required for children under eight years old unless they are at least 4ft 9in tall.

➡ High-occupancy vehicle (HOV) lanes marked with a diamond symbol are reserved for cars with multiple occupants, sometimes only during rush hours.

➡ Unless otherwise posted, the speed limit is 65mph on freeways, 55mph on two-lane undivided highways, 35mph on major city streets and 25mph in business and residential districts.

➡ At intersections, U-turns are permitted unless otherwise posted.

➡ Except where indicated, turning right at red lights after coming to a full stop is permitted, although intersecting traffic still has the right of way.

➡ At four-way stop signs, cars proceed in the order in which they arrived. If two cars arrive simultaneously, the one on the right has the right of way. When in doubt, wave the other driver ahead.

→ When emergency vehicles (such as police, fire or ambulance) approach from either direction, be sure to carefully pull over to the side of the road.

→ If a police car is pulled off on the shoulder of the road, drivers in the right-hand lane are legally required to merge left, as long as it's safe to do so.

→ It's illegal to carry open containers of alcohol inside a vehicle, even empty ones. Unless containers are full and still sealed, store them in the trunk.

→ California has strict anti-littering laws; throwing trash from a vehicle may incur a $1000 fine.

PARKING

Parking is plentiful and free in small towns and rural areas, but is generally scarce and expensive in big cities. You can pay municipal parking meters and centralized pay stations with coins (eg quarters) or sometimes credit or debit cards. When parking on the street, read all posted regulations and restrictions (eg street-cleaning hours, permit-only residential areas) and pay attention to colored curbs, or you may be ticketed and towed. Expect to pay at least $2.50 per hour or $25 overnight at a city parking garage. Flat-fee valet parking at hotels and restaurants is common in cities; make sure you tip the valet attendant at least $2 when your keys are handed back to you.

FUEL

→ Gas stations in California, nearly all of which are self-service, are everywhere, except in national parks and remote desert and mountain areas.

→ Gas is sold in gallons (one US gallon equals 3.78L). At the time of research, the cost for midgrade fuel was more than $4.

Driving Problem-Buster

What should I do if my car breaks down? Call the roadside emergency assistance number of your car-rental company or, if you're driving your own car, your automobile association. Otherwise, call information (🖉411) for the number of the nearest towing service or auto-repair shop.

What if I have an accident? If it's safe to do so, pull over to the side of the road. For minor fender benders with no injuries or significant property damage, exchange insurance information with the other driver and file a report with your insurance provider as soon as possible. For major accidents, call 🖉911 and wait for the police and emergency services to arrive.

What should I do if I am stopped by the police? If you are stopped by the police, be courteous. Don't get out of the car unless asked. Keep your hands where the officer can see them (eg on the steering wheel). For traffic violations, there is usually a 30-day period to pay a fine; most matters can be handled by mail. Police can legally give roadside sobriety checks to assess if you've been drinking or using drugs.

What should I do if my car gets towed? Call the police nonemergency number for the town or city that you're in and ask where to pick up your car. Towing and hourly (or daily) storage fees can quickly total hundreds of dollars.

What if I can't find anywhere to stay? If you're traveling during summer and/ or holiday periods, always book accommodations in advance, as beds fill up fast. If you're stuck and it's getting late, it's best not to keep driving on aimlessly – just pull into one of those ubiquitous roadside chain motels or hotels.

California Playlist

Surfer Girl Beach Boys

(Sittin' On) The Dock of the Bay Otis Redding

California Love 2Pac & Dr Dre

California Dreamin' The Mamas & the Papas

California Phantom Planet

California Gurls Katy Perry featuring Snoop Dogg

ROAD TRIP WEBSITES

Driving Conditions & Traffic

California Department of Transportation (www.dot.ca.gov) Highway conditions, construction updates and road closures.

511.org (www.511.org) San Francisco Bay Area traffic updates.

go511.com (www.go511.com) LA and Southern California traffic updates.

Automobile Clubs

American Automobile Association (www.aaa.com) Emergency roadside assistance (24-hour), free maps and travel discounts for members.

Better World Club (www.betterworldclub.com) Ecofriendly auto-club alternative to AAA.

Maps

Google Maps (http://maps.google.com) Free online maps and driving directions.

National Park Service (www.nps.gov/state/ca/index.htm) Links to individual park sites for road condition updates and free downloadable PDF maps.

Road Rules

California Department of Motor Vehicles (www.dmv.ca.gov) Statewide driving laws, driver's licenses and vehicle registration.

BEHIND THE SCENES

SEND US YOUR FEEDBACK

We love to hear from travelers – your comments help make our books better. We read every word, and we guarantee that your feedback goes straight to the authors. Visit **lonelyplanet. com/contact** to submit your updates and suggestions.

Note: We may edit, reproduce and incorporate your comments in Lonely Planet products such as guidebooks, websites and digital products, so let us know if you don't want your comments reproduced or your name acknowledged. For a copy of our privacy policy visit lonelyplanet.com/privacy.

ACKNOWLEDGMENTS

Climate map data adapted from Peel MC, Finlayson BL & McMahon TA (2007) 'Updated World Map of the Köppen-Geiger Climate Classification', *Hydrology and Earth System Sciences*, 11, 163344.

Cover photographs: Front: Napa Valley Vineyards, Dennis Frates/Alamy; Back: Golden Gate Bridge, Andrew Zarivny/Shutterstock

Illustration pp58-9 by Michael Weldon

THIS BOOK

This 1st edition of *San Francisco Bay Area & Wine Country Road Trips* was researched and written by Sara Benson, Alison Bing, Beth Kohn and John A Vlahides. This guidebook was produced by the following:

Associate Product Director Angela Tinson

Senior Cartographer Alison Lyall

Book Designer Katherine Marsh

Assisting Book Designers Jennifer Mullins, Virginia Moreno

Cover Researcher Campbell McKenzie

Thanks to Shahara Ahmed, Sasha Baskett, Brendan Dempsey, James Hardy, Darren O'Connell, Katie O'Connell, Martine Power, Wibowo Rusli, Luna Soo, Clifton Wilkinson

OUR STORY
A beat-up old car, a few dollars in the pocket and a sense of adventure. In 1972 that's all Tony and Maureen Wheeler needed for the trip of a lifetime – across Europe and Asia overland to Australia. It took several months, and at the end – broke but inspired – they sat at their kitchen table writing and stapling together their first travel guide, *Across Asia on the Cheap*. Within a week they'd sold 1500 copies. Lonely Planet was born.

Today, Lonely Planet has offices in Melbourne, London and Oakland, with more than 600 staff and writers. We share Tony's belief that 'a great guidebook should do three things: inform, educate and amuse'.

INDEX

A

accidents 123
accommodations 13, *see also individual destinations*
Alcatraz 19, 58-9, **58-9**
art 60

B

Baltimore Canyon 78
Bass Lake 21
Bear Flag Republic 38
bird-watching 79
Bodega 46
Bodega Bay 46, 115-16, **117**
Bohemian Hwy 45
Bolinas 20, 22, 78-9
breakdowns 123
breweries 78
business hours 13

C

Calistoga 29, 31-2, 91-3, **31**
car rental 12, 120-2
cars, *see* driving
cell phones 12
Chez Panisse 20
classical music 67-9
climate 12
Coleman Valley Rd 45

000 Map pages
000 Photo pages

cookery courses 95, 112
Corte Madera 78
costs 13
cycling 75

D

driver's licenses 120
driving 12, 120-4
Dry Creek Valley 48, 101

E

East Fort Baker 20
emergencies 12, 68

F

Ferry Building 19, 64
flag, California 38
fog 75
food 13, *see also individual destinations*
Freestone 45, 105, 106
fuel 12, 123

G

galleries, *see* museums & galleries
gardens, *see* parks & gardens
gas 12, 123
GLBTI travelers 48, 66
Glen Ellen 22, 38, 97-9
Golden Gate Bridge 9, 54, 74, **8-9**, **76-7**
Guerneville 47, 107-11

H

Hawk Hill 19
Healdsburg 47-8, 111-14
hiking
    Bodega Head 115
    Marin Headlands 72-3
    Muir Woods National Monument 78
    Sonoma Coast State Beach 117
horseback riding 74, 115
hot-air ballooning 93
hot springs 32

I

insurance 120
internet access 12

J

Jenner 46, 118

K

kayaking 112
Kenwood 40, 97-9

L

Larkspur 78
Lazy Bear Weekend 48
lighthouses 21, 81
live music 66-7
London, Jack 39

M

maps 122
Marin County 19-22, 70-81, **18**, **72-3**
Marin Headlands 19-20, 22, 70-4
Mexico, travel to/from 122
Milk, Harvey 52
mobile phones 12
money 13
motorcycles, see driving
mountain-biking 73-4
mud baths 32
Muir Woods 20, 78, **80**
museums & galleries
  Asian Art Museum 55
  Exploratorium 55
  MH de Young Museum 54
  Mission murals 60
music 124, see also live music

N

Napa 22-3, 27, 83-7
Napa Valley 23-33, 82-93, **26**, **86**, **90**

O

Oak Hill Farm 38
Oakville 27-8, 88
Occidental 45, 105-7
opening hours 13
opera 67

P

parking 10, 123
parks & gardens
  Bartholomew Park 40
  Crissy Field 56
  Golden Gate Park 54
Petrified Forest 32
petrol 12, 123
Point Reyes 21-2, 79-81

Point Reyes National Seashore 22, 80-1
Point Reyes Station 79-80

R

redwoods 20, 32, 45-7, **8**, **80**, **109**
reserves, see parks & reserves
road distances 121
road rules 122-3
Russian River area 46, 48, 99-118, **44**, **100**
Rutherford 28, 88

S

Safari West 32
safety 122-3
San Francisco 10-11, 19, 52-69, **56**, **62**, **10-11**, **16**, **53**
  accommodations 60-1
  dangers & annoyances 68
  drinking & nightlife 64-5
  entertainment 66-7
  festivals & events 57, 60
  food 63-4
  history 52-4
  information 68-9
  shopping 67-8
  sights 19, 54-7
  transport within 69
  walking tours 62
  websites 69
Sausalito 20, 74-8, **21**
sea lions 22
seals 22, 46
Sebastopol 45, 102-4
Silverado Trail 33
Sir Francis Drake Blvd 21, 78
Sonoma 37-8, 94-7
Sonoma Coast State Beach 46, 117
Sonoma Valley 22, 35-41, 94-101, **36**, **94**
spas 32

state parks & reserves
  Armstrong Redwoods State Reserve 46-7
  Bale Grist Mill & Bothe-Napa Valley State Parks 91
  Jack London State Historic Park 39
  Robert Louis Stevenson State Park 33
  Sugarloaf Ridge State Park 98
Stevenson, Robert Louis 29, 32, 33
St Helena 28-9, 89-90

T

telephone services 12
tipping 13
Traintown 37
transportation 13, 120-4

V

Vallejo, General Mariano Guadalupe 38

W

weather 12
websites 13, 124
whale-watching 22, 46, 115
wi-fi 12
wildlife watching 22, 79
wine 23
wineries
  Alexander Valley 101-2
  Dry Creek Valley 101
  Napa Valley 23-33, 82-3
  Russian River area 45, 47-8, 100-2
  Sonoma Valley 22, 35-40, 93-7

Y

Yountville 27

OUR WRITERS

SARA BENSON

After graduating from college, Sara jumped on a plane to California with just one suitcase and $100 in her pocket. She has bounced around the Golden State ever since, including in the Sierra Nevada, where she worked as a seasonal park ranger. The author of over 50 travel and nonfiction books, Sara also coordinated Lonely Planet's *California* guide. Follow her adventures online at www.indietraveler. blogspot.com, www.indietraveler.net and @indie_ traveler on Twitter.

Read more about Sara at: www.lonelyplanet.com/ members/Sara_Benson

ALISON BING

Over 10 guidebooks and 20 years in San Francisco, author Alison Bing has spent more time on Alcatraz than some inmates, become an aficionado of drag and burritos, and willfully ignored Muni signs warning that "safety requires avoiding unnecessary conversation."

JOHN A VLAHIDES

John A Vlahides co-hosts the TV series *Lonely Planet: Roads Less Travelled*, screening on National Geographic Channels International. John studied cooking in Paris, with the same chefs who trained Julia Child, and is also a former luxury-hotel concierge and member of Les Clefs d'Or, the international union of the world's elite concierges. He lives in San Francisco, sings tenor with the Grammy-winning San Francisco Symphony, and spends free time biking SF and skiing the Sierra. For more, see JohnVlahides. com, twitter.com/JohnVlahides.

Read more about John at: lonelyplanet.com/ members/johnvlahides

BETH KOHN

A lucky long-time resident of San Francisco, Beth lives to be playing outside or splashing in big puddles of water, and there's always a California atlas stashed in her red pickup truck in case a back road looks particularly promising. An author of Lonely Planet's *Yosemite, Sequoia & Kings Canyon National Parks*, *Mexico* and *California* guides, you can see more of her work at www.bethkohn.com.

31901056360078

Published by Lonely Planet Publications Pty Ltd
ABN 36 005 607 983
1st edition – May 2015
ISBN 978 1 74360 705 3
© Lonely Planet 2015   Photographs © as indicated 2015
10 9 8 7 6 5 4 3 2 1
Printed in China

Although the authors and Lonely Planet have taken all reasonable care in preparing this book, we make no warranty about the accuracy or completeness of its content and, to the maximum extent permitted, disclaim all liability arising from its use.